# Made in God's Image

# Made in God's Image

## *The Incest Survivor's Embodied Journey from Deicide to Resurrection*

Sumer Bingham Musick

*Foreword by Jane Grovijahn*

PICKWICK *Publications* • Eugene, Oregon

MADE IN GOD'S IMAGE
The Incest Survivor's Embodied Journey from Deicide to Resurrection



Pickwick Publications
An Imprint of Wipf and Stock Publishers
199 W. 8th Ave., Suite 3
Eugene, OR 97401

www.wipfandstock.com

PAPERBACK ISBN: 979-8-3852-1013-8
HARDCOVER ISBN: 979-8-3852-1014-5
EBOOK ISBN: 979-8-3852-1015-2

Cataloguing-in-Publication data:

Names: Bingham Musick, Sumer, author. | Grovijahn, Jane, foreword.

Title: Made in God's image : the incest survivor's embodied journey from deicide to resurrection / Sumer Bingham Musick ; foreword by Jane Grovijahn.

Description: Eugene, OR : Pickwick Publications, 2026 | Includes bibliographical references and index.

Identifiers: ISBN 979-8-3852-1013-8 (paperback) | ISBN 979-8-3852-1014-5 (hardcover) | ISBN 979-8-3852-1015-2 (ebook)

Subjects: LCSH: Psychic trauma—Religious aspects—Christianity. | Psychic trauma—Religious aspects. | Feminist theology. | Incest victims—Mental health. | Women—Mental health.

Classification: BT732.7 .B52 2026 (paperback) | BT732.7 (ebook)

VERSION NUMBER 04/27/26

For Jenn.
May you walk again in the truth that you are made in God's image.

# Contents

# Foreword

TRAUMA INVENTS ITS OWN connective tissue. When I was pioneering waters that threatened to drown my own divine being in a body gutted by violation, little did I know or could have imagined my initial work of holy God-filled survival would connect me to Dr. Bingham Musick.

What a privilege it is for me to introduce this work by Dr. Bingham Musick. Twenty-five years ago I embarked upon a similar journey in lands that were barren and unforgiving. I could not have known then that a commitment to the theological voice of survivors would have brought me full circle to this place where I get to see some of the fruitful harvest of those hard fought gains in scholarship. Given our larger social reality, it is a feat of justice and raw courage to advance the theological agency and power of women, but even more so provocative to create spaces of divine revelation in the lives and actions of abuse survivors.

This distillation of hope, agency, and comprehensive scholarship is sorely needed now and adds deep insight to an ongoing discovery about the value and spiritual wisdom in the lives of those whose embodied childhoods were filled with terror and trauma. The author embeds us into that variegated ground gently, with great care and Divine prodding. In the final pages the author offers a humble hope: that the witness of her work will be the hands and feet of God in a sexually traumatized world. I see it going much deeper in fact. Her work carries depth and compassion in her integration of conversation partners and theological prompts, some sourced in social scientific scholarship, some with survivors' own reflections and, perhaps most refreshingly, a dance into the divine mysteries enfleshed in Jesus's own journey of dying and being resurrected. It is an invitation into the power and beauty in and through our own broken bodies. Her work invites us into the visceral context of Incarnation as we name and appropriate our own embodied losses. Her work is a testament, a very embodied witness to the perduring enigma of Divine presence and power, now no longer muted by the unspeakable harm done in the sexual violations put upon us.

She helps illumine the reality of creativity in chaos, inviting us to procure a reinvention of ourselves beyond the status of victim and claim our residence in the life of God. This is the power of Resurrection offered in Dr. Bingham Musick's work. In my early years as a scholar, I was determined to bring my own struggle with sexual violation into the theological arena where the holiness of survival could sing from the hard ground of wounds and fearful silences. This work evocatively brings hope and power to the surface where something emerges from the wounding, connecting us in visceral ways to the Image of God that does not negate the violation, but somehow, dwells within it. It offers what I would call a welcome and heavy holiness.

As a survivor and trauma scholar, I am not only validated by her work but challenged to integrate her work around my own, calling me back to my deepest self. I congratulate her for this deep dive into the nexus of what often lives in flesh without language and frequently carries the impossible burden of robbing us of what should be ours by birth: radical inclusion in the unfolding mystery of Divine communion and delight. Her work draws out what is shattered into the realm of the eternal and prompts us to pull deeply from our embodied stories as part of the great commissioning of Christ, predicated, she says, on the entirety of his wounded body. Now that is a theology worth living; she offers a God whose Presence cannot be diminished or detoured by trauma.

I eagerly invite you, the reader, into this condensing of lifetimes carried by so many abuse survivors who dare to articulate an ancient claim on the Divine. It carries a significant sensibility of grace that attunes our ear for God in a new and necessary way. We are the blessed and broken ones, who carry the Incarnation from within the viscosity of violation, but now shining with an irrepressible livingness of God.

Theologizing from and with sexually abused bodies comes from a place of power, and it initiates a hunger for a taste of the Holy rarely imagined. I invite us all into this feast, to sit at this table, and to relish how we, as the broken ones, divulge God's own power precisely through the pain and terror we have carried for our lifetimes.

Dr. Jane Grovijahn
Professor Emerita, Theology and Spiritual Action
Our Lady of the Lake University, San Antonio, Texas

# Acknowledgments

In 2020 I taught an undergraduate class called Spiritual Care and Trauma. It was an experimental class designed to help me flesh out the inner workings of what would eventually become this book. The class was small and contained only seven students. Incidentally, it turned out that the class self-selected. Every single student divulged that they were survivors of trauma. The majority were survivors of sexual violence. For sixteen weeks we learned the lingo surrounding trauma, grappled with God-questions related to suffering, and pondered what "post-traumatic growth" looks like both individually and within a community.

While we did all the typical things you would expect in a college course, the real magic happened between the lines. As these seven insightful young adults began to ascribe language to their journeys, they continually returned to the body. Inside the classroom they scraped the surface of how trauma continues to live within their flesh. They discovered why words often failed to capture their reality. They discussed hard theological concerns that they had been too afraid to voice. They agreed (and often disagreed) on topics related to forgiveness, boundaries, and belonging. Above all else, they each began to confront harmful lies that they had embodied about their own identity.

It should be noted that I am not a therapist. I am a theologian. Our course conversations were not a dumping ground in which we rehashed traumatic experiences. Rather, we discussed how to care for the wounded soul. We identified individual and community needs and how those unmet needs manifest in day-to-day life. We wrapped our conversations around spiritual frameworks and theological methods designed to move people and communities toward wholeness. We learned about and embodied spiritual care practices that sought to remind wounded bodies of their sacredness.

Several years later this class is still the most meaningful and humbling course I have ever had the privilege to teach. I learned more about the grace and beauty of God in this short time than all my years of prayer had taught me. I witnessed forgiveness, belonging, love, and grace in abundance. They may not know it, but they helped me discover these things within myself. It is their stories, and many more, that are written between the lines of this work. It is the voices that have been silenced for too long that I feel compelled to acknowledge with each keystroke.

A multitude of academic conversation partners helped me readily witness and formulate the beauty that unfolded in my course and subsequent research. Notably, Dr. Jane Grovijahn's work provided powerful language for both myself and my students as we examined the spiritual wounds inflicted by trauma. Dr. Marcia Mount Shoop's work on embodiment opened the window to the many different experiences the body can hold. I have also been shaped by Pamela Cooper-White, Judith Herman, David Tombs, Monica Coleman, Bessel van der Kolk, and countless others who have laid the foundation for meaningful trauma research.

In addition to these voices, I would be remiss if I did not acknowledge the mentors that guided me along the way. Dr. Bryan Froehle, Dr. Mary Carter Waren, and Sr. Pat Doody were conversation partners that dutifully read, reread, and guided my work. Laurie Sandblom and Rev. Dr. Karen Reed are the unsung heroes whose friendship and support have been instrumental. My colleagues at the University of Pikeville, my alma mater and home, have invested in me financially, professionally, and personally in ways that exceed expectations. I offer my heartfelt gratitude to Dr. Burton Webb, Dr. Lori Werth, Dr. Thomas Hess, and Dr. James Browning.

I owe my deepest appreciation and acknowledgment to my family. To my mother-in-law, Brenda Musick, who provided extra babysitting and boundless love to my children while I wrote, I offer my heartfelt gratitude. Most importantly, my husband, Rev. Dr. Rob Musick, has been my sanctuary and support throughout the development of this work. He has invested countless hours proofreading numerous drafts. He has enthusiastically engaged in long, rambling, late-night theological discussions that helpfully challenged and sharpened my presuppositions. He has encouraged me to keep writing, even when I wanted to quit. His presence, together with that of our children, has served to anchor me to the preeminently important work of joy, laughter, and play.

This network of support helped me encounter the narrative of Jesus anew. Along the way, I have learned the insurmountable truth that even the sexually traumatized body is made in God's image.

# Introduction

LIFE IS FULL OF unimaginable tragedy. It probably does not take a great stretch of memory to call to mind a pain so profound that it takes your breath away. Moments of grief, fear, sorrow, and longing permeate the human experience. When we encounter the more painful moments in life, solace is often sought and found in community. The profound loss of a loved one, the terror at facing a terminal diagnosis, the trauma of losing everything in a natural disaster . . . the weight of burdens like these become somewhat easier to bear if others stumble with us through the pain. While outpourings of love do not take away the suffocating pain we might encounter, they do serve as an anchor which tethers us to the reality that we are not alone. Providing food after a funeral, holding the hand of a sick loved one, mucking out a home after flood waters have violently swept away years of memories . . . these are all acts of love that bear witness to the suffering of our neighbors.

While many pains and sorrows in life are more transparent tragedies, what about those pains that are shrouded in silence and shame? Imagine, for a moment, a scenario that is shockingly prevalent in our society. Consider a young child full of hope, laughter, and curiosity. Like so many others, she is born into a family whose primary job is to love and care for her. And yet, as is so often the case, her family is also tasked with navigating their own pasts full of trauma and pain. Generations of trauma compound upon this family. Addiction and abuse are the untold family secrets that shape the behavior of the adults to whose care she has been entrusted. The result is often a volatile home where the child must provide care for herself and others. The worries about food and utility bills consume the mind of the young child as she, too, learns to navigate the complexities of addiction and abuse. Once full of vitality and creativity, her energy becomes directed at ensuring her own safety and discovering silent ways to cope with ongoing oppression. It is no surprise that by the age of nine, her innocence is stolen by a sexual predator. She becomes part of the one in four girls who will be sexually abused by the age of eighteen.[1]

With any luck, this child will grow up to become an adult who must heal in a world where it is socially taboo to talk about her experiences. How are we to provide love to people who have endured pain so profound that scholars have likened it to death?[2] How can solace be sought or found when the trauma that one has encountered is not discussed? How can we best love someone whose sense of safety and being has been shattered during childhood? How can we bear witness to this prevalent, yet hidden, pain in our society?

This research dives deeply into the pain of child sexual abuse in the form of incest. It is an attempt to bear witness and create space for the voices that have endured a trauma so profound that they struggle to describe and make sense of it all. Child sexual abuse in the form of incest is a type of harm that attacks the very core of one's being. It mutates one's understanding of self into a *thing* that feels inherently filthy. How can one understand life after enduring this continual death? What type of wound does this experience inflict, and can one ever truly heal? Who is God and where was God during the abuse? Where is God now as so many learn to live in violated bodies? In the aftermath of childhood sexual abuse which shakes and alters the substance of one's being, is it possible to know, build a relationship with, or access God's love? These are practical theological questions rooted and grounded in experience.

## TERMINOLOGY AND THEOLOGICAL FRAMING

The creation of this research has been an academic, spiritual, and personal journey. As I have sought deeper understanding and healing from my own experiences of childhood sexual abuse, enduring questions have emerged. As my understanding of God and my relationship with my own body has evolved, I have come to realize that sexual violence violates the body in ways far more intimately connected to our sense of personhood than other forms of violence. It attempts to oppress the substance of who we are as people.

Personal narratives, therapeutic techniques, and scientific research converge to ascribe language and understanding to the pain endured. Child

1. Briere and Scott, *Principles of Trauma Therapy*, 9.
2. Rambo, *Spirit and Trauma*, 7.

sexual abuse, however, is often overlooked as a theological problem. The reality of this theological problem is made known in the stories of those who have been able to articulate their abuse. Empowered voices bring to light the oppression, shame, and spiritual wounds inflicted and offer a beacon of companionship and hope to others finding their way through the darkness.

This work is intended for adult female survivors of childhood sexual abuse in the form of incest and any in the Christian community who wish to join our journey toward wholeness. Despite its shocking prevalence in society, this is a taboo topic and the word "incest" is often avoided. Incest is a jarring word. It carries a heavy burden of shame and disgrace, convincing those who have endured it that they are less than and alone. The only way to heal shame is to shine a light on it and destroy the narrative of isolation. For this reason, I will refer to child sexual abuse in the form of incest as simply "incest" throughout the remainder of the work.

Those who have endured incest are victims, survivors, and children of God. Healing is not linear, and there is no term that encompasses the totality of mindsets and experiences of incest. Therefore, the words "survivor" and "victim" will be used interchangeably. In a very real sense of the word, those who have endured incest are victims. Many do not survive, and their stories, often untold, emerge between the lines of this work. Likewise, many of us remain and must learn to live with the violence written upon our flesh. Because of this, the word "survivor" is also used. It is my fierce hope to acknowledge the harm caused and offer a spiritual pathway for wholeness. In truth, both words have their limitations. I aim to make my very best effort to honor children and women's painful experiences of incest.

This practical theological work utilizes a hermeneutic of rape that brings together embodied theology and David Tracy's work in his *Analogical Imagination*. In other words, it is a way of doing theology that begins with the embodied experience of incest. It critically reflects upon that experience and brings it into dialogue with both the social sciences and the experiences of Jesus.[3] Tracy argued that Jesus was the "prime analogue" or the experience through which all other experiences can be more deeply understood. By utilizing a hermeneutic of rape that reads the biblical text

3. This definition of practical theology is informed by Swinton's understanding of practical theology as a critical reflection on the praxis of the church in dialogue with theology and other sources of knowledge. It is also informed by Heitink's definition that practical theology is an empirically oriented reflection on the Christian praxis of faith in mediation with modern society. Tracy, *Analogical Imagination*; Crisp, "Reading Scripture," 23–42.

through the lens of sexual violence, Good Friday, Holy Saturday, and Resurrection Sunday will offer new insights into the reality of incest.

How one knows God is fundamentally altered because of incest. The expectation and beliefs in a child's understanding of God are met with the reality of enduring harm. Amid this cognitive dissonance, a death of how one knows God occurs. The bio-psycho-social impact of incest is accompanied by rape culture and dysfunctional family systems that work together to inflict a compounded and oppressive harm. It is in this space of oppression and violation that the knowledge and experience of God become woven into bodily reality. The ultimate promise of hope and resurrection can be discovered in the sexually abused body, which is revelatory of God.

## ORGANIZATION

The social sciences provide a firm foundation upon which to explore the nature of life that continues beyond trauma. The prevalence of abuse, mind-body response, and long-term impact of the experience are all explored in social scientific literature. The scientific bodily understandings of trauma teach that experience lingers, the body keeps the score, and those who endure carry scars. The social sciences, however, do not provide insight into the spiritual wounds accrued through this form of trauma.

This research is grounded in the belief that "human beings are genetically potentiated for partnership with God."[4] Although the experience of incest inflicts incredible harm, the truth that all beings are made in God's image remains. Taking an embodied theological approach, this work deeply explores the bodily experience of incest to discern God's presence. In doing so, one can honor and empower even the most violated and broken pieces of one's identity. Jane Grovijahn notes that "daring to do theology from a sexually abused body begins with need—a deep unforgiving need."[5] This need for spiritual understanding, healing, and community moves this research forward.

Chapter 1 will establish the compounded harm associated with incest using a social scientific perspective. The terms "trauma" and "incest" will be defined and statistics regarding the prevalence of abuse will be named. Additionally, the bio-psycho-social impact of incest will be explored. Rape culture historically undergirds continual acts of violence, and so a brief history of this

4. Fowler, *Faith Development*, loc. 543 of 1515.

5. Grovijahn, "Theology as an Irruption into Embodiment," 29.

insidious violence will be outlined. In addition, a connection will be made between rape culture and predominant biblical interpretations. Together, this information provides the context for understanding incest.

Chapter 2 answers the questions "Who is God, and how do we know God?" Psychoanalysts and developmental psychologists argue that our faith and understanding of God are shaped by complex internalized relationships during childhood. The development of God's image will be discussed in dialogue with child sexual abuse. What does it mean to be made in God's image for incest survivors? Historical interpretations of *imago Dei* will be brought into dialogue with developmental psychology to address these questions. It will be argued that a *deicide*, or death of how we know God, occurs.

Death, however, is not the end. Chapter 3 will explore the literature surrounding embodied theology and illuminate how the sexually abused body is revelatory of God. The social location of the sexually violated body will give way to a deeper understanding of embodied ethics that prompt systemic change in society. It is through feeling the body amid tragedy, ambiguity, and creativity that God's presence becomes fully known. In the aftermath of incest, God must be known differently—through a violated body.

While chapters 1, 2, and 3 offer the theoretical and social scientific foundation for understanding incest theologically, chapters 4, 5, and 6 explore the experience analogically. Chapter 4 will bring the concept of deicide into dialogue with the crucifixion of Jesus. The death of Jesus's safety, innocence, and body will be correlated with the deaths experienced by those who endured incest. Jesus experienced a loss of safety and innocence as his disciples betrayed him and he was publicly stripped and beaten. Furthermore, the death of Jesus's body is coupled with social death on the cross. The experience of Jesus's death is compared to incest survivors, and this research will emphasize the significance of a hermeneutic of rape.

Chapter 5 will examine Holy Saturday. The silence and darkness after the crucifixion and before the resurrection are profoundly important spaces that include concepts of dissociation, crisis of faith, and uncertainty. Although we eagerly await the resurrection, it is not wise to rush to a new life without remaining in liminality. This chapter will identify some of the painful questions that occur during one's journey and discuss how to carry on without answers.

After darkness comes new life. Jesus's story does not end with his crucifixion and burial. The resurrection provides hope and emphasizes the beauty of life over death. Still, Jesus is not resurrected without wounds. Learning how to live in a body that holds the experience of death is hard and holy work. Jesus, however, offers a framework for considering this endeavor. Reflection upon the resurrected and wounded body brings a transformation of one's physicality, memory, and identity. Chapter 6 brings these ideas into dialogue with survivor narratives.

Written for survivors and those in the Christian community who journey with us, this work moves incest into the light so that it can be healed. In conjunction with the Great Commission, chapter 7 outlines practical ways in which communities can help heal the wounds of incest. Still yet, there is significant work to be done. The spiritual wounds inflicted by incest can no longer fester in silence. While this research acknowledges the profound harm that occurs, it also offers a robust theological understanding of the experience and provides avenues of resurrection. So, who is God, and how does one know God after the experience of incest? This work dares to theologize from the sexually abused body to discover what wisdom such bodies hold.

# 1

# Context

*Whoever has ears, let them hear:*
*The pounding of my feet as they pulled me toward a predator*
*screaming senseless rage about my worth laced with my soul.*
*The pitch black beam of hate berating my belonging,*
*My voice swallowed.*

*Whoever has ears, let them hear:*
*The cloud of breath catching in front of me with each sob*
*The clink of freezing cold gravel biting my shifting palms*
*The acidic bile forcing its way from my strangled cry.*
*My panicked wail.*

*Whoever has ears, let them hear:*
*The frenzied flutter of my heart, fiercely clinging to life*
*The relentless roar of my panic as I return to my ruined body*
*The silent search for safety, the small sounds that strangle my soul*
*Why am I so wrong?*

*Whoever has ears, let them hear:*
*I still listen to every word, silently starving for a sanctuary*
*I still hear violence and fear, chaos and rape,*

*Enduring ruptured memory rebounding through my body*
*I never knew silence could sound so shattering.*

*Whoever has ears, let them hear.*

## DEFINING TRAUMA

Trauma has become a popular word. Most recently, it has been used in pop psychology to denote difficult experiences or persistent stresses. It has become a catch-all term layered with harmful misconceptions that painfully negate real trauma. Trauma is, by its very nature, "unbearable and intolerable."[1] Bessel van der Kolk notes that trauma impacts "the core of who we are . . . it changes not only how we think and what we think about, but also our very capacity to think."[2] It is an unbearable, intolerable, all-consuming experience that demands attention.

The *Diagnostic Statistical Manual* (*DSM*) defines trauma as an event. It is caused by a stressful occurrence that includes "actual or threatened death, serious injury, or sexual violence."[3] Trauma can be caused via "direct personal exposure, witnessing of trauma to others, and indirect exposure through trauma experience of a family member or other close associate."[4] The Center for Anxiety Disorders further defines trauma as "a psychological, emotional response to an event or an experience that is deeply distressing or disturbing."[5]

Trauma physically changes the brain and interrupts the natural processes of the mind resulting in phenomena such as dissociation, alexithymia, and repression.[6] Trauma also interrupts the instinctual fight, flight, and freeze mechanisms designed to ensure self-preservation.[7] Judith Herman defines trauma as an "affliction of the powerless. At the moment of trauma, the victim is rendered helpless by overwhelming force."[8] She goes

1. Van der Kolk, *Body Keeps the Score*, 1.
2. Van der Kolk, *Body Keeps the Score*, 21.
3. American Psychiatric Association, *Desk Reference to the DSM-5*, 271.
4. Pai et al., "Posttraumatic Stress Disorder in the DSM-5," 7.
5. Rosen, "What Is Trauma."
6. Van der Kolk, *Body Keeps the Score*, 92–93, 190, 273.
7. Levine, *Waking the Tiger*, 24.
8. Herman, *Trauma and Recovery*, 33.

on to note that trauma continually tries to discredit or render the victim invisible and powerless.[9]

Trauma is not confined to the individual, however. It can also be understood sociologically and is often conceptualized as a collective experience that impacts global events and politics. Herman notes that the integration and study of trauma have historically been driven by political force. Her work emphasizes the episodic amnesia of trauma studies and underlines the importance of history and society in the healing process. She notes that three significant periods of Western history have resulted in the study of trauma via hysteria, shell shock, and rape trauma syndrome.[10] Traumatic experience is made possible, in part, by faulty systems that silence and oppress. Increasing social awareness of trauma can thus lead to healing within society as it invariably impacts policies and laws.[11] Understanding trauma sociologically prompts reflection and awareness of policies and the social structures that promote oppression, justice, reconciliation, and violence.

While professionals from a variety of social science disciplines have offered numerous frameworks for conceptualizing and treating trauma, religious traditions have also sought to understand trauma (particularly sexual trauma) in ever more relevant ways. Theologians like Monica Coleman have produced theologies born from their own traumatic pain. Coleman noted the failings of the church in light of her own rape and wrote a communal guidebook on how the church community can and should respond to trauma, particularly sexual violence.[12] Some theological works expand upon this notion, emphasizing a trauma-sensitive theology and grace. They offer constructive criticism for the current failings of the church to address trauma adequately.[13] Part of this response is developing a hermeneutic of rape when exploring biblical texts. Pamela Cooper-White, Beth Crisp, Renita Weems, and Elaine Heath have all produced works that depict the importance of reading the biblical text through the lens of the sexually

9. Herman, *Trauma and Recovery*, 8.

10. Herman, *Trauma and Recovery*, 9. These correspond respectively with the republican anti-clerical movement in France; WWI, WWII, and the Vietnam War; and the feminist movement of Western Europe and North America.

11. Alexander, *Trauma*.

12. Coleman, *Dinah Project*.

13. Jones, *Trauma and Grace*; Baldwin, *Trauma Sensitive Theology*.

abused.[14] These theologians all wrestle with the concept of trauma from practical perspectives—trauma is terrible . . . but what can be done about it?

Doing something about trauma depends, in part, on how one conceptualizes the wound itself. In Shamanic practices throughout the world, trauma is understood as a fragmentation of the soul. When one experiences an overwhelming event, the soul may become separated from the body. When the soul fails to reintegrate properly, it results in what the Western world has dubbed trauma. Shamanic traditions understand trauma as an injury to the very core of our being—the soul. This soul loss can be healed by trained shamans who draw upon a variety of resources, which may include drumming, herbal substances, dancing, chanting, and community support.[15]

In Buddhist meditation practices trauma is not seen as a "diagnosis" or "problem," but rather a natural response to a painful event. Trauma is not something that defines the totality of a person. It is not an experience to overcome or push away. Instead, the traumatic response is something that one must meet with compassion and openness. This can be particularly difficult, however, as it is so overwhelming and isolating.

Christian theologian Shelly Rambo notes, "For those who survive trauma, the experience of trauma can be likened to a death. But the reality is that death has not ended."[16] For Rambo, trauma is an open wound that has not been integrated.[17] She offers reflections on remaining in this liminal space by likening it to Holy Saturday. Others offer a theology of hope. Dan Allender's work emphasizes the evil and sinful nature of abuse and frames recovery as a war in which one must overcome shame to accept the beautiful, abundant life God intended for humanity.[18] The spiritual wound inflicted by incest is characterized in this work as *deicide* or the death of how one knows God. This deicide is brought about by the compounded harm of the biological, psychological, social, and cultural experiences of incest, which result in a malformed understanding of the self as made in God's image.

14. Cooper-White, *Cry of Tamar*; Crisp, "Reading Scripture"; Weems, *Battered Love*; Heath, *We Were the Least of These*.

15. Levine, *Waking the Tiger*, 58–59; Eliade, *Shamanism*, 215–58.

16. Rambo, *Spirit and Trauma*, 7.

17. Rambo, *Spirit and Trauma*, 7.

18. Allender, *Wounded Heart*.

## STATISTICS

Child sexual abuse occurs at an alarming rate.[19] Instances of sexual violence are notoriously underreported and underprosecuted, with incest falling at the severe end of that reality. Incest is a form of severe trauma that is closely linked to familial dysfunction. It is defined as "sexual contact or behavior occurring between related or quasi-related individuals . . . [it is] considered a form of child abuse when the perpetrator is older, physically bigger and stronger, and/or holds a position of power or authority over the victim."[20] It often occurs in conjunction with other forms of familial abuse such as addiction; mental illness; verbal, physical, or emotional abuse; and neglect and abandonment.[21] Usually, incest occurs in dysfunctional homes where parents or guardians contribute to a lack of boundaries, safety, and belonging for the child. Allender calls incest a crime against "the abused person's body and soul" that rips away the safety and innocence of childhood.[22] Statistically, it is not an exaggeration to say that everyone knows someone who has been victimized, even though they might not be aware of it. Despite its prevalence within society, it is still considered a taboo topic that remains shrouded in shame.

Every nine minutes, Child Protective Services substantiates or finds evidence for a claim of childhood sexual abuse.[23] According to the Department of Justice Child Maltreatment Report, 67 percent of all victims of sexual assault reported to law enforcement agencies were juveniles. The FBI's National Incident-Based Reporting System (NIBRS) determined that

19. Several barriers exist to providing consistent and accurate data for incest victims. Most notably, the various reporting agencies that produce regular statistical reports do not differentiate neatly among the data. For example, the FBI's annual report does not differentiate between adult and juvenile victims of sexual violence. While the Department of Justice produces an annual report on victimology, the latest report exploring child maltreatment was published in 2000. Furthermore, the Department of Health and Family Services studies child maltreatment more broadly, including incidences such as neglect and domestic violence. Incidences of child sexual assault, particularly in the form of incest, tend to be underreported to law enforcement and other agencies, further skewing the data. It is with these limitations in mind that the available data is considered. Snyder, *Sexual Assault of Young Children*; Finkelhor et al., *Sexually Assaulted Children*, 2.

20. Courtois, "Healing the Incest Wound," 497.

21. Courtois, "Healing the Incest Wound," 497.

22. Allender, *Wounded Heart*, 36.

23. RAINN, "Children and Teens: Statistics."

one in every seven victims of sexual violence is under the age of six and one-third of all sexual assaults involve a child under the age of twelve.[24]

Reports of child sexual abuse suggest that approximately 25–35 percent of women are sexually abused as children.[25] Indeed, girls are six times more likely than boys to become victims, and females make up 86 percent of all victims of sexual assaults.[26] Children are most vulnerable between the ages of seven and thirteen, while most girls are abused between the ages of twelve and fourteen. The National Center for Victims of Crime (NCVC) notes that 63 percent of women who suffered sexual abuse by a family member experienced other instances of sexual assault after the age of fourteen.[27]

The Department of Justice determined that nearly 77 percent of all sexual assaults involving a child occurred within the home of the victim or perpetrator.[28] The data shows that the younger the child, the more likely it is that the perpetrator is a family member. Ninety-six percent of all offenders are male, and 92 percent of all juvenile victims are abused by a family member or close acquaintance.[29] Only 3 percent of offenders are strangers to the victim.[30] Unfortunately, only 27 percent of cases result in arrest.[31] When the perpetrator is a family member or close acquaintance, they are more likely to be cleared. This is due to a myriad of reasons including victim intimidation, protection of family systems, cultural shame, and taboo.[32]

Statistical data can help discern God's will by providing clear direction to "the least of these" in society. The reality of these statistics, then, is preeminently important. Approximately 25 percent or one in four women are sexually abused as children. That means one in four women in the grocery store line, one in four women at the movie theatre, one in four women in a classroom, and one in four women in the church pews have endured

24. Snyder, *Sexual Assault of Young Children*, 2, 12.

25. Briere and Scott, *Principles of Trauma Therapy*, 9.

26. Snyder, *Sexual Assault of Young Children*, 3. It should be noted, however, that male sexual assaults are even more underreported.

27. National Center for Victims of Crime, "Child Sexual Abuse Statistics."

28. Snyder, *Sexual Assault of Young Children*, 6.

29. Snyder, *Sexual Assault of Young Children*, 8.

30. Snyder, *Sexual Assault of Young Children*, 10. See table 6.

31. Snyder, *Sexual Assault of Young Children*, 11.

32. Snyder, *Sexual Assault of Young Children*, 12.

the oppressive violence of child sexual abuse. Of these, approximately 92 percent are victims of incest.

## BIO-PSYCHO-SOCIAL IMPACT OF CHILD SEXUAL ABUSE

While there is still much to learn, the long-term impacts of such experiences have been extensively studied. Perhaps the strongest and most widely known indicator of trauma's long-term impact is the Adverse Childhood Experiences (ACE) survey. Vincent Felitti, Robert Anda, and their colleagues in 1995 developed this survey in a study funded by the Centers for Disease Control. Originally beginning as a study on obesity, Felitti and his colleagues discovered that the more adverse childhood experiences an individual had, the more likely they were to develop chronic illness.[33]

The ACE survey asks a series of ten questions categorized into three main categories: abuse, neglect, and household dysfunction. Felitti's work discredited the age-old adage that people should just "get over it" or "move on" from traumatic experiences. As one's ACE score increases so does the risk for negative health and behaviors. In short, the higher the ACE score, the greater the risk for cardiovascular disease, cancer, addiction, gastrointestinal disorders, autoimmune disorders, muscular and skeletal pain, depression, anxiety, and other health problems. For example, a person with an ACE score of four is 390 percent more likely to develop chronic obstructive pulmonary disease than a person with an ACE score of zero. Individuals with higher ACE scores are thirty to fifty times more likely to attempt suicide than those with lower scores. Felitti and his team determined that "more than two-thirds of suicide attempts could be attributed to adverse childhood experiences."[34]

While the statistics regarding child sexual abuse and ACE scores are unsettling, the embodied reality of the experience is even more so. The body itself becomes an inescapable place fraught with terror, confusion, and uncertainty. The mind often lacks the capacity to process the event and memories continue to live within the body. Post-traumatic experiences often make individuals feel as if they are going crazy, living a double life, or as if they are dead inside. It can often be difficult to understand what is happening within the body during a post-traumatic response.

33. Felitti, "Adverse Childhood Experiences and Adult Health," 44–47.

34. Felitti, "Adverse Childhood Experiences and Adult Health," 44–47.

It is a misconception that memory exists solely within the mind. Bodies are hard-wired to store memory throughout. A complex array of neurons exists throughout the entire body. These neurons continually transmit messages between and within the brain and body via electrical impulses and chemicals. These messages control heart rate, breathing, pain, and other critical functions.[35] All the while, the body and brain learn from events. Memories are formed and recalled when familiar neuron patterns are reactivated.[36] Neurons and memory, then, exist throughout the body. For those who have experienced incest, the trauma is enfleshed.[37]

Long after a traumatic experience, a "trigger" can reactivate familiar neuron patterns, reminding one of abuse. This trigger can result in a cascade of experiences such as accelerated heart rate, shallow breathing, headaches, or feeling the same physical sensations that occurred during the trauma. Snapshots of the original traumatic memory may intrude and replay in one's mind, nightmares may disrupt sleep, or one may feel hypervigilant with no conscious awareness of why. This can result in increased anger, agitation, or risky behavior such as sexual promiscuity, self-harm, or drug use in attempts to quiet the pain. It may also manifest as dissociation as the brain seeks to protect itself from harm.

Dissociation has been called the "essence of trauma."[38] When an experience is too traumatic and overwhelming, it becomes fragmented. The emotions, sounds, smells, thoughts, and physical sensations take on a life of their own and, if not processed, will continue to intrude into the present moment long after the event has occurred.[39] The mind's job is to protect itself at all costs. When experience and memory become too much, areas of the brain will shut down. This can result in dissociation and speechlessness as areas of the brain associated with self-awareness and language go offline.[40] When a

35. Woodruff, "What Is a Neuron?"

36. Queensland Brain Institute, "How Are Memories Formed?"

37. Mount Shoop, *Let the Bones Dance*, 49.

38. Van der Kolk, *Body Keeps the Score*, 66.

39. Van der Kolk, *Body Keeps the Score*, 66.

40. Van der Kolk, *Body Keeps the Score*, 92–93. The brain contains a "mohawk of self-awareness" that provides a physical sense of where we are, how we are, and what we are. In other words, midline brain structures coordinate emotions and thoughts with sensory input from neurons. In a study of eighteen individuals with PTSD resulting from early life trauma, it was discovered that these midline structures were minimally active. Neuroscientists determined that these patients had learned to "shut down the brain areas that transmit the visceral feelings and emotions that accompany and define terror."

trigger occurs and these midline structures go offline, individuals may feel as if they are watching their lives through a window. The world acquires a surreal quality, as if they are experiencing it through a film. Others may feel nothing at all as their mind has disengaged from their bodily sensations. The result is often a deadened capacity to feel fully alive.[41]

Dissociation and depersonalization are further deepened by the phenomenon of alexithymia, or the inability to attribute words to feelings.[42] The experience of trauma is so difficult that many individuals have difficulty sensing what is happening within the body. They have learned to disconnect to survive. As a result, it becomes difficult to explain what they are feeling, be it physical or emotional.[43] For those who have experienced incest, the events are, quite literally, unspeakable.[44]

During this speechless horror, survivors of incest must learn to navigate a body that remembers their abuse. The body becomes an inescapable crime scene. At any given moment an unprocessed trigger can send the body into a cascade of responses disrupting ordinary life and returning one to the center of their worst experiences. Mount Shoop notes that "sexual trauma shatters any sense of safety a person used to feel. The shattered pieces penetrate the depths of who we are. We are not safe in life's most intimate spaces; we are not safe in our own bodies."[45]

As a result of this ongoing and compounded harm, individuals who have experienced incest may develop "complex deformations of identity [that result in a] malignant sense of the self as contaminated, guilty, and

---

Unfortunately, it is this same "mohawk of self-awareness" in the brain that helps govern a sense of self and helps individuals understand who they are. This distance from one's sense of self is a form of dissociation, known more specifically as depersonalization.

41. Van der Kolk, *Body Keeps the Score*, 94.

42. Van der Kolk, *Body Keeps the Score*, 100–101.

43. Van der Kolk, *Body Keeps the Score*, 43–44. Trauma may cause Broca's area, the portion of the brain responsible for language, to literally go offline. MRI scans of traumatized people show Broca's area as inactive when a traumatic memory is recalled. These scans, taken during the midst of a trigger, are not very different from Broca's area among stroke victims. Van der Kolk notes: "Even years later traumatized people have enormous difficulty telling other people what has happened to them. Their bodies reexperience terror, rage, and helplessness, as well as the impulse to fight or flee, but these feelings are almost impossible to articulate. Trauma by nature drives us to the edge of comprehension, cutting us off from language."

44. Van der Kolk, *Body Keeps the Score*, 43–44.

45. Mount Shoop, "Body-Wise," 243.

evil."[46] They may feel insignificant or less than, or place unrealistic demands on themselves in addition to experiencing a heightened sense of perfectionism, loss of voice, and loss of control.[47]

## RAPE CULTURE

The bio-psycho-social experience of sexual violence is compounded by the presence of rape culture. Rape culture has been defined as a "subset of values, beliefs, and behaviors in a society that trivializes or normalizes sexual violence, including rape."[48] Characteristics of rape culture include, but are not limited to, the normalization of sexually aggressive language (locker room talk, slut shaming, catcalling, etc.), victim blaming, silence, media distortions, and cover-ups. In a rape culture, society comes to accept that this violence is an ordinary part of life. Stories about sexual violence are often negated, and the focus is placed on understanding or justifying the perpetrator's actions. Attempts to upset this status quo often result in shaming, victim-blaming, community rejection, punishment, and/or subjugation. This compounded harm results in what Gina Messina-Dysert calls a "second rape."[49] The presence of this compounded harm in modern society is informed by a long and arduous history that can easily be tracked.

Studies show that rape spans time and geography. Throughout history, women have suffered the most when their sexuality is controlled, their contribution to society is restricted, and the punishment for the violation is weak.[50] Most literature reviews the history of rape and rape culture chronologically by examining legal codes, religious narratives, court documents, and media representations. Among this literature three major trends emerge:

- Sexually violated women are understood as objects rather than people
- Sexually violated women are silenced and preference is given to the perpetrator
- Death is seen as preferable to living a life with sexual impurity

46. Courtois, "Healing the Incest Wound," 470.
47. Saha et al., "Narrative Exploration," 108, 111.
48. Dictionary.com, "Rape Culture."
49. Messina-Dysert, *Rape Culture*, 1.
50. Lalumiere et al., *Causes of Rape*, loc. 176 of 5610.

## Objectification

In many societies, women have historically been understood as the property of men. Deuteronomy 22 states, "If a man meets a virgin who is not engaged, and seizes her and lies with her, and they are caught in the act, the man who lay with her shall give fifty shekels of silver to the young woman's father, and she shall become his wife. Because he violated her he shall not be permitted to divorce her as long as he lives" (Deut 22:28–29).[51] Similarly, a second-millennium BCE Assyrian law states that if a virgin is taken by force, then her father may choose to give her to her perpetrator for marriage or receive payment in the form of a fine.[52]

In both examples, monetary compensation is provided to the woman's father and, if the father chooses, the woman will marry her perpetrator. Having lost her virginity (and thus her purity) in the act of rape, the woman would not be desirable for other marriages. Her guardian could choose to arrange a marriage with her abuser or accept payment for the damages. Restitution was made to the guardian, not to her, underlining the reality that she is more closely understood as an object rather than a person. If a woman was raped, then the violation was understood as an attack against or theft of her male guardian's possessions.[53]

Women understood as objects for men is evident in the biblical story of the rape of King David's concubines. In this story, Absalom is staging a political coup to overthrow his father, David. He is counseled to "go into" his father's concubines in the sight of all of Israel to symbolically show the people that what was once David's is now his. The text states in 2 Samuel:

> Then Absalom said to Ahithophel, "Give us your counsel; what shall we do?" Ahithophel said to Absalom, "Go in to your father's concubines, the ones he has left to look after the house; and all Israel will hear that you have made yourself odious to your father, and the hands of all who are with you will be strengthened." So they pitched a tent for Absalom upon the roof; and Absalom went in to his father's concubines in the sight of all Israel. (2 Sam 16:21–28)

Scholars largely approach this passage from a contextual perspective and interpret this as a political act that "affirm[s] in the eyes of the public that

51. All scripture from the New Revised Standard Version; see also Lalumiere et al., *Causes of Rape*, loc. 227 of 5610; Propp, "Kinship in 2 Samuel 13," 39–53.

52. Lalumiere et al., *Causes of Rape*, loc. 228 of 5610.

53. Lalumiere et al., *Causes of Rape*, loc. 238 of 5610.

Absalom has asserted his rights as king."[54] This "public relations event" establishes Absalom's dominance over David.[55] Some scholars argue that Absalom's actions were done to convince the people that David was dead. A. A. Anderson and Ernst Wurthwein note that "it was forbidden for a son to take his father's wife, at least while the father was alive."[56] Absalom, then, violates two laws: he "enter[s] the sexual property not only of another man, but of his father."[57]

Modern scholarship largely interprets this story as a political act without considering the sexually violent elements emblematic of rape culture. This dominant interpretation underlines the objectification of women. The concubines are considered possessions of David, and they are used as objects in a political ploy. Their thoughts and feelings are not considered. They are not named. These women are not seen as made in God's image. Indeed, for both the original author and modern interpreter, they barely register as people.

The attitude that women are the objects or possessions of men is an attitude that persists well into Western thought. Medieval European court documents show harsh punishments for the rape of unmarried or virgin women. However, victims' families were responsible for prosecution, making it unlikely that anyone except the wealthy would pursue legal charges. Wealthy fathers could seek payment in the form of a fine and so rape laws were designed to protect the father's "assets." The notion that payment to one's husband or father could result in the dismissal of justice underlines the dehumanization of women. Women have historically been understood as objects, assets, and/or political bargaining chips rather than people. This aspect of rape culture, which endures throughout history, emphasizes society's refusal to see women as made in God's image.

## Silence

Rape culture also silences and discredits the stories of women who have experienced this violence. This can be witnessed in the rape of Dinah in Gen 34. The text states:

54. Robinson, *1 and 2 Samuel*, 239.
55. Peterson, *First and Second Samuel*, 215.
56. Anderson, *2 Samuel*, 214; see also Wurthwein, *Text of the Old Testament.*
57. Messina-Dysert, *Rape Culture*, 14.

> Now Dinah the daughter of Leah, whom she had borne to Jacob, went out to visit the women of the region. When Shechem son of Hamor the Hivite, prince of the region, saw her, he seized her and lay with her by force. And his soul was drawn to Dinah daughter of Jacob; he loved the girl, and spoke tenderly to her. So Shechem spoke to his father Hamor, saying, "Get me this girl to be my wife." (Gen 34:1–4)

Later in the story, Jacob and Dinah's brothers approve this marriage if Shechem and his men agree to be circumcised. Jacob's sons then attack Shechem's men, slaughter them, and abduct the women and children. Dinah, having been in Shechem's house this entire time, returns home. Jacob is furious over the actions of his sons, fearing that their actions will bring war and disaster upon them. "But they said, 'Should our sister be treated like a whore?'" (Gen 34:31).

In this text, Dinah is silenced. At no point in the story is her voice made known. She is never consulted during her rape, in the arrangements made regarding her marriage to Shechem, and during the attack on Shechem's people. Dinah's experience as a raped woman becomes a political bargaining chip. Even her brothers, who are seemingly attempting to avenge her purity, do not consult her. She is further silenced in acts that perpetuate violence.

Similar to the story of David's concubines, modern scholarship often minimizes Dinah to focus instead on the men in the story.[58] Shechem has been understood as a symbol reflecting the conquest of the promised land and a man willing to do the "right thing" by marrying Dinah.[59] Although he violated marriage custom by having sex with Dinah without parental consent, Lyn Bechtel claims that his "overall action . . . is one of honor" because he tried to repair the situation.[60]

While many try to defend the honor of Shechem, others focus instead on blaming Dinah. It is not difficult to find research claiming that Dinah was asking for it.[61] G. C. Aalders states:

> We can surmise that [Dinah] also had some natural desires to be seen by the young men of the city as well . . . . It was disturbing that Dinah would so flippantly expose herself to the men of this pagan

58. Messina-Dysert, *Rape Culture*, 8.
59. West, "Rape of Dinah," 151; Coats, *Genesis*, 234.
60. Bechtel, "What If Dinah Is Not Raped?," 31.
61. Carmichael, *Women, Law, and the Genesis Traditions*, 42.

> city. . . . As a matter of fact, Dinah was far more at fault for what had happened than anyone else in the City of Shechem.[62]

The interpretive claims that glorify Shechem and vilify Dinah are characteristic of rape culture. She is silenced, and modern interpretation places the weight of shame and blame upon her.

This trend has been all too familiar in history. In the seventeenth century, women were prosecuted for sexual offenses more than men, despite being the victims. Adultery, fornication, and illegitimate pregnancies ranked highest in court documents. Adult women who had been raped were often labeled as fornicators and held responsible for the assaults "on the grounds that they were sexually insatiable."[63] For cases of incest, the victim was often considered an accomplice. Lalumiere notes that the perceived "respectability of the alleged rapist was a powerful defense" often allowing for the dismissal of charges.[64] Just as the status of Shechem justifies his "honorable action," women are still, well into the twenty-first century, silenced and blamed when victimized by "good" men.[65]

In the nineteenth century, this victim blaming was built into the very definition of rape. Victorian England defined rape as "a brutal act of violence usually committed in a public place on an apparently respectable woman who was previously unknown to her assailant and had done nothing even to acknowledge his presence."[66] This definition does not account for the circumstances that encompass most acts of sexual violence. Rarely does a stranger leap from the dark to attack in a public setting. It is evident from the research that most attacks occur in private and by someone who is familiar. This definition (albeit dated) encompasses still-persistent attitudes about sexual violence that discredit and silence the lived reality of women. It makes possible the persistent interpretation that Dinah (and, by extension, others like her) must have been asking for it. Why else would a woman go out to socialize?

62. Aaldars, *Genesis*, 154, 159, as quoted in Messina-Dysert, *Rape Culture*, 9.

63. Lalumiere et al., *Causes of Rape*, loc. 375 of 5610.

64. Lalumiere et al., *Causes of Rape*, loc. 395 of 5610.

65. Consider, for example, the popular modern cases of Brett Kavanaugh and Brock Turner.

66. Conley, "Rape and Justice in Victorian England," 525.

## Impurity

Levitical law contains a holiness code that emphasizes a separation between the clean and unclean, the sacred and the profane, and the holy and the common.[67] The laws promote rituals that separate one from sin and uncleanliness. In short, "what is profane and unclean temporarily disqualifies a person from coming into the presence of God."[68] Although Leviticus provides an extensive list of what is clean and unclean, scholars have long debated where the line is drawn for some of the more arbitrary boundaries.[69] Some, like Mary Douglas, have speculated that cleanness is a matter of "wholeness or normality."[70] Scholars agree, however, on the fact that the law demands a line be drawn between the sacred and the secular. In Levitical law, being unclean is a barrier when worshiping God.

Leviticus notes that after intercourse a man and woman must bathe with water and will be unclean until evening.[71] Deuteronomy says:

> If a man happens to meet in a town a virgin pledged to be married and he sleeps with her, you shall take both of them to the gate of that town and stone them to death—the young woman because she was in a town and did not scream for help, and the man because he violated another man's wife. You must purge the evil from among you. But if out in the country a man happens to meet a young woman pledged to be married and rapes her, only the man who has done this shall die. Do nothing to the woman; she has committed no sin deserving death. This case is like that of someone who attacks and murders a neighbor, for the man found the young woman out in the country, and though the betrothed woman screamed, there was no one to rescue her. If a man happens to meet a virgin who is not pledge to be married and rapes her and they are discovered, he shall pay her father fifty shekels of silver. He must marry the young woman, for he has violated her. He can never divorce her as long as he lives. (Deut 22:23–29)

Implicit in these laws is the understanding that to prove rape it must be witnessed and/or interrupted by the woman's screams. While there is no law explicitly stating that a raped woman becomes ritually impure, one's

67. Kaiser, "Book of Leviticus," 999.

68. Kaiser, "Book of Leviticus," 999–1000.

69. Kaiser, "Book of Leviticus," 1000.

70. Douglas, *Purity and Danger*, 53.

71. Lev 15:16–18.

virginity was preferential in marriage regulations. If a man married a woman who he later found out was not a virgin, she could be stoned to death.[72] Furthermore, rape often left women living isolated and alone. For example, after Tamar's half-brother Amnon rapes her in 2 Sam 13:1–21, she is "a desolate woman" who wept loudly and placed ashes on her head. When Absalom raped David's concubines, David returned and "kept them in confinement till the day of their death, living as widows" (2 Sam 20:21).

While this violence leads to isolation, it is also historically associated with uncleanness and impurity. In prominent saintly lore, it is better to die than be raped. The life of Saint Maria Goretti is a relatively recent example, taking place in Italy in 1902. When Maria was twelve years old, Alessandra Serenelli attacked her. He demanded that she let him rape her or be killed. She accepted death and he stabbed her fourteen times. She later died from an infection from one of the stab wounds. She used her dying breaths to apologize for making her mother sad and to forgive her attacker. She is the youngest canonized saint in the church.

Similarly, the rape of St. Lucretia results in her demise. She is known as a chaste and virtuous woman. Sextus Tarquinius is lustful and he seizes her by force. He threatens her with death as he tries to rape her. She is not threatened by his sword, and she refuses to submit. He then threatens her with shame and disgrace, "saying that when she was dead he would kill his slave and leave him naked beside her, that she might be said to have been put to death in adultery with a man of base condition."[73] Faced with this shame, she submits. She then tells her husband and father what happened, claims her innocence, and commits suicide to redeem her honor.[74]

These stories point to larger trends in virgin martyr legends. Countless stories of women who die to protect their purity can be found. Their deaths are often gruesome and exceedingly violent. Messina-Dysert outlines it well:

> Saints Margaret and Cecilia were boiled; Saint Agnes was beheaded; Saint Katherine was mangled by spiked wheels; Saints Agatha and Barbara both had their breasts torn from their bodies, and Saint Apollonia had her teeth wrenched out. Saint Ursula was butchered in a mass martyrdom along with eleven thousand other

72. See Deut 22:21 (NIV).

73. Torjesen, *When Women Were Priests*, 139; Messina-Dysert, *Rape Culture*, 16.

74. Messina-Dysert, *Rape Culture*, 16.

> virgins and Saint Lucy gouged out her own eyes to discourage any man from being tempted by her.[75]

These women choose virgin deaths to demonstrate their love for God. They die horrifically but their hymens remain intact. As a result, they are canonized and celebrated. Jerome went as far as to say, "Although God is able to do all things, he cannot raise up a virgin after a fall."[76] Rape is understood then to separate one from God. A life lived with sexual impurity is characterized by objectification, silence, shame, and inaccessibility to God. In these stories, life after sexual violence is not worth living.

## RAPE CULTURE AND CHILD SEXUAL ABUSE

The umbrella of rape culture informs child sexual abuse. Western society has been remarkably slow in recognizing the lasting trauma inflicted by child sexual abuse, and attempts to understand the phenomenon have often resulted in more understanding for perpetrators than those abused. Historically institutions have sought to minimize the publicity surrounding claims of child sexual abuse and have failed to hold perpetrators accountable, effectively silencing and diminishing the experiences of those who have endured this harm.[77] The shame embodied during this compounded harm can be crippling.

The interest in child sexual abuse has ebbed and flowed over time, with periods of interest typically coinciding with greater social anxieties.[78] The entry of women into the workforce, a rise in divorce rates, debates about child labor, and increases in juvenile delinquency have, historically, pushed the conversation into the light. Most recently, broader concerns regarding the breakdown of the American family system have surfaced.[79]

Society has generally agreed that sexual acts with a child under the age of ten are harmful and perverse.[80] Sexual encounters with young girls were generally regarded as pathological in the nineteenth century. However,

75. Messina-Dysert, *Rape Culture*, 19.

76. Jerome, "Epistle 22:5," in *Select Letters of St. Jerome*; Messina-Dysert, *Rape Culture*, 16.

77. Mintz, "Placing Childhood Sexual Abuse."

78. Mintz, "Placing Childhood Sexual Abuse."

79. Mintz, "Placing Childhood Sexual Abuse"; Pleck, *Domestic Tyranny*; Gordon, *Heroes of Their Own Lives.*

80. Robertson, "Age of Consent Laws," item #230.

instances of abuse were difficult to prove. Girls were expected to adhere to particular stereotypes and display their naivete and innocence in their language.[81] If this did not happen then young girls were often cast as willing participants who seduced their perpetrators. While the abuse itself was difficult to prove, seemingly open-and-shut cases in which children contracted venereal diseases were often rationalized by blaming their illness on dirty toilet seats.[82]

Historically, some argued that when a girl physically matures, at the age she begins menstruating, then she is old enough to give consent. This understanding placed "consent" around the age of twelve. It was not until the twentieth century that lawmakers began considering the sexual development and maturity of children. The age of consent was eventually raised to sixteen. Despite placing a specific age on the issue of consent, however, older girls (approximately between the ages of twelve to sixteen) were expected to fight back and show marks of their resistance.

In the early to mid 1900s, the social hygiene movement focused on promoting unified standards of sexual morality to reduce physical and psychological illness in society. This movement argued that sexual desire developed throughout one's lifetime and began in infancy. In *The Mental Hygiene of Childhood*, William Alanson White stated that "people are loath to see and to acknowledge that the infant of two, three, and four years of age has sexual feelings."[83] Freud famously identified five stages of psychosexual development where children focused on different parts of their bodies as "pleasure zones." The stages outlined by Freud were oral (ages zero to two), anal (ages two to three), phallic (ages three to six), latency (ages six to puberty), and genital (beyond puberty).[84]

This focus on psychosexual development and hygiene colored perceptions of child sexual abuse. Studies on those who had experienced incest focused on how children behaved during the encounters rather than on the impact it had on their lives. Referring to a study conducted in 1937, Robertson notes that researchers Bender and Blau were "struck by the fact that their subjects did not resist 'and often play[ed] an active or initiating role'

81. Mintz, "Placing Childhood Sexual Abuse."

82. Mintz, "Placing Childhood Sexual Abuse."

83. White, *Mental Hygiene of Childhood*, 113–14; Robertson, *Crimes Against Children*, 150.

84. Robertson, *Crimes Against Children*, 150.

in their encounters with adult men."[85] They then concluded that children did not "deserve completely the cloak of innocence with which they have been endowed."[86]

This led to the treatment of children by obviously faulty adult standards. Joseph Weiss and his colleagues dubbed children as "accidental victims" or "participant victims." Accidental child victims only experienced the sexual act once—usually by a stranger—received no payment or remuneration, and told their parents immediately after. Participant victims knew the offender and likely experienced sexual acts multiple times, received some type of remuneration (candy, money, movie tickets, etc.), and kept the experience secret.[87] This attitude created space for the argument that children could seduce their abusers.

Despite these theories of psychosexual development, society at large continued to support the innocence of children. Post–WWII anxieties in the 1940s and 1950s generated discourse on how to protect one's child from sexual predators. Some argued that a child's physical appearance triggered men's sexual instincts. "Scanty clothing" worn by young girls took the blame as it invited assaults. Perpetrators were considered mentally ill and treatable, lacking in sexual maturity. They were easily "seduced" by young girls whose dress or behavior did not match the socially conceived standards of childhood innocence. In response, school districts distributed information to families educating them about "stranger danger" and appropriate behavior for children.[88] People came to fear the unknown rapist, which served to insulate perpetrators within the family.

Simultaneously, parents grew wary of reporting sex crimes for fear that the court process would destroy their child's innocence. The possibility of recounting the sexual experience in front of a crowded courtroom was dangerous. For example, "Littleton claimed that parents believed that such a 'harrowing' experience would render a child 'unfit for the future, [and unwilling] to go back to school,' and would leave him or her 'marked for all time.'"[89] Robertson points out that they feared their child would be "ruined."

85. Bender and Blau, "Reaction of Children," 513–14; Robertson, *Crimes Against Children*, 153.

86. Bender and Blau, "Reaction of Children," 500–518; Robertson, *Crimes Against Children*, 153.

87. Robertson, *Crimes Against Children*, 152–53; Weiss et al., "Study of Girl Sex Victims," 1–3.

88. Robertson, *Crimes Against Children*, 154–57.

89. Robertson, *Crimes Against Children*, 156.

Additionally, the 1900s failed to acknowledge the systems that perpetuated such abuse. While there is much scholarly debate in regard to the causes of rape, there is a consensus among researchers that rape is most prevalent when there is "warfare, gender antagonism, constraints on women's sexuality, and generally low status of women [in society]."[90] In the case of child sexual abuse, systems that perpetuate disproportionate power dynamics, silence, and constraints on sexuality have historically been ripe with instances of such abuse. Furthermore, men who rape are generally antisocial, tend to engage in high mating efforts, show sexual arousal to violent material, and rape more often when the costs are low.[91]

## The Co-Morbidity of Family Dysfunction

By the 1980s, it became generally accepted that "intrafamilial sexual abuse is a problem which generally involves the whole family unit."[92] Incest does not happen in isolation but rather in conjunction with dysfunctional family systems. Stern and Meyer developed a three-type classification system to help analyze this dysfunction: possessive-passive, dependent-domineering, and incestrogenic.

The possessive-passive classification is characterized by a dominant patriarchal husband that controls a passive wife and dependent children. These family systems are often financially stable and conventional, and have a strong adherence to traditional gender roles. The father controls nearly all aspects of life, sometimes with force, and is "manipulative, domineering, and unpredictable [while presenting] a public persona of a conventional and responsible family [man]."[93] Pelletier and Handy note that "they tend to select immature, ineffective spouses who can be kept financially dependent and isolated."[94]

A strong and domineering woman and an inadequate man characterize the dependent-domineering type. In this situation, the father has little power in the family, is incapable of meeting his spouse's emotional needs, and looks to his wife for support and nurturing. The mothers in this dynamic are "assertive, educated, and [more] capable than the wives of

90. Lalumiere et al., *Causes of Rape*, loc. 219 of 5610.

91. Lalumiere et al., *Causes of Rape*, loc. 3665 of 5610.

92. Pelletier and Handy, "Is Family Dysfunction More Harmful," 51.

93. Pelletier and Handy, "Is Family Dysfunction More Harmful," 51.

94. Pelletier and Handy, "Is Family Dysfunction More Harmful," 51.

possessive husbands. [They] tend to be colder and more rejecting toward their children."[95]

The incestrogenic type is characterized by chaos and includes "two very dependent adults who cannot meet each other's overwhelming needs." In this situation, the parents are inadequate as both parents and spouses, show poor impulse control, and have poor judgment. Family roles tend to be confused with very little structure.[96]

In each of these models, dysfunction characterizes the marital relationship. The imbalance of power creates an unsafe environment in which generational boundaries can break down. Children are often triangulated in parental conflicts or placed in parental positions. There is no consideration for childhood development, children are often exposed to situations that are far beyond their developmental capacity to grasp, and they are frequently placed in roles where they must meet inappropriate expectations. As a result, children develop "'pseudomature' behaviors in order to prevent the disintegration of the family."[97]

This weight of holding the household together results in an intense commitment to the family. The broken boundaries can result in "enmeshment and sometimes pathological dependence" that can be incredibly difficult to escape. Issues of control, fear, and loss permeate the child's reality. Communication is poor in families where incest has occurred. "Denial is an intrinsic part of the family process, and family members expend a considerable amount of energy keeping 'secrets' and maintaining 'myths' which are perceived as essential."[98] This silence is accompanied by closed systems in which family members are actively discouraged from engaging people outside of the family. Pelletier and Handy powerfully state, "As the daughter lives with the secret of the abuse, the fate of the family rests almost entirely on her shoulders in a climate of isolation, coercion, and possible violence."[99]

In addition to the bio-psycho-social impact of incest, the umbrella of rape culture that informs modern perceptions of abuse, and the dysfunctional family system through which it takes place, the traumatized self becomes characterized by overwhelming feelings of shame and guilt. It is

95. Pelletier and Handy, "Is Family Dysfunction More Harmful," 51–52.

96. Pelletier and Handy, "Is Family Dysfunction More Harmful," 52.

97. Pelletier and Handy, "Is Family Dysfunction More Harmful," 53.

98. Pelletier and Handy, "Is Family Dysfunction More Harmful," 54.

99. Pelletier and Handy, "Is Family Dysfunction More Harmful," 54.

no surprise that avoidance and rationalization are common coping mechanisms.[100] It may be extremely difficult to accept that a deeply trusted person is responsible for such violations. Dan Allender notes what these rationalizations may sound like:

> The abuser was abused as a child. He had a hard background that would have made anyone a little crazy. He was going through a terrible time with his wife and was lonely. He drank to the point that he didn't know what he was doing, so how could he be held accountable? He did so many wonderful things for people, how can I be angry for just one failure?[101]

These excuses are defense mechanisms put in place to protect the mind from the reality of harm. While enduring the abuse, they are life-saving tactics. Over time, however, these same defense mechanisms become wounds that need to heal. The reality is more pain.

To place guilt and blame where it is due is enormously difficult. It means acknowledging the depth of harm and betrayal by someone whose job it is to protect, nurture, and love the child. It risks violence, alienation, and the utter loss of the system that has been most ingrained into one's very being—the family. Most of all, it risks making the shame and degradation that one has come to feel visible for all to see.

This agony goes far beyond the experience of the traumatic event itself. It permeates every pore of one's being, seeping into the very fabric of one's identity. Experiences are held in the tissues and cells as they wreak havoc upon relationships, bodies, and memories. And yet, much of therapeutic intervention ignores the reality of the body as it silently screams to tell its story. Silence and shame continue to characterize the experience of trauma, which violates the sanctity of the body, disrupts memory, sabotages relationships, upends one's identity, and murders the reality of the *imago Dei.*

100. Saha et al., "Narrative Exploration," 108.

101. Allender, *Wounded Heart*, 36.

## 2

# God Image

*A cold*
*Uneven*
*Splintered floor*
*A grizzly*
*Unnurtured*
*Unfinished foundation*
*A tattered sheet*
*A broken voice*
*Questions.*
*Silence.*

*Who are you, God, that you do not answer?*
*He has constant access.*
*Praying, joyous, gifted,*
*"God's got a plan for him," they all say*
*The day after he peels off my shirt and makes me touch him.*

*A foggy mirror*
*Hollow eyes*
*Empty. Shaking. Terrified.*
*Confused.*

*I don't believe.*
*I cry.*
*I search.*
*Do I matter? Do you exist? Am I loved?*
*Obviously not.*
*Still, I pray.*

Every person's encounter with God is unique. Culture, family, life experience, and expectations color our perceptions of God. The God encountered during childhood is perceived differently as one enters a spiritually mature adulthood. A child who discovers God in a stable, supportive, and loving environment will likely have a different relationship with God than the troubled adolescent who seeks God from a place of desperation. While each of these unique encounters with God points to an enduring and holistic model of divinity, they also point to a deeper question about how our God image is formed. Who *is* God and how do we come to know God?

Developmental psychologists and pastoral care providers alike have persistently argued that one's self-image informs one's God-image. Janet Ruffing notes:

> There is always a correlation between our self-image and our image of God. As we undergo the process of growth and development, our sense of ourselves forms and reforms on the basis of our experiences. Automatically, our self-image sets up a correlative image-pair with who God is to us, whether explicit or not.[1]

Self-image, and thus God-image, is formed in complicated and dynamic ways throughout life. A child's relationship with their parents provides the foundation for this self-image and simultaneously shapes the way God is understood. Much like the unfolding of life and the development of personality, however, this development of God-image is not neatly constructed. While scholars gravitate toward a psychoanalytic understanding, they are in agreement that God is formed out of a sense of belonging and joy as well as disappointments and idealizations.

This chapter reviews major psychoanalytic and attachment theories regarding the formation of God-image. A child's God-image is shaped by parental perceptions and is informed by self-image as one grows older. This

1. Ruffing, *Spiritual Direction*, 127.

God-image changes over time, and the formation of one's faith calls forth certain expectations of God at various stages of life. This developmental understanding of imaging God has profound implications for those who have experienced incest. Parental relationships, understanding of self, and unmet expectations of God culminate in the death of how one knows God. And yet, theological teachings articulate time and time again that humanity is made in God's image. What does that mean for the survivor of incest?

## THEORIZING THE FORMATION OF GOD-IMAGE

While Freud had a notably derogative view of religion, his theories provided a jumping-off point for future psychoanalysts. He believed that the belief in God was built upon a child's perception of parents manifested during the resolution of the Oedipal phase. Ana-Maria Rizzuto, in her work *Birth of the Living God*, expanded upon Freud's initial ideas via case studies and interviews.

In Rizzuto's work, she notes the importance of religion and God-image in the human experience. Whether or not one identifies as theistic, there is nevertheless a belief in who God is. She distinguishes between God's concept and image. The God concept is "an intellectual, mental-dictionary definition of the word 'God.'"[2] God-image, however, is "a psychological working internal model of the sort of person that the individual imagines God to be."[3] This understanding of the God-image is made and remade continually in life both consciously and unconsciously as we face ordinary experiences such as birth, adolescence, love, marriage, loss, and death. She notes:

> The very pressure of living makes us rework, over and over again, consciously and unconsciously, the memories of those we encountered at the beginning of our days—the time of the heroic, mythic reality of childhood. The fantasy of the child certainly adds color, drama, glamour, and horror to the insignificant moments as well as to the real tragedies of everyday life. It is out of this matrix of facts and fantasies, wishes, hopes, and fears, in the exchanges with those incredible beings called parents, that the image of God is concocted.[4]

2. Lawrence, "Measure the Image of God," 214.
3. Lawrence, "Measure the Image of God," 214.
4. Rizzuto, *Birth of the Living God*, 7.

Childhood creativity does not only inform God-image. God is also found in the family. Rizzuto states:

> Most of the time [God] is offered by the parents to the child; he is found in everyday conversation, art, architecture, and social events. He is presented as invisible but nonetheless real. Finally, most children are officially introduced to the "house of God," a place where God supposedly "dwells" one way or the other. That house is governed by rules very different from any others; the child is introduced to ritual, to the official behavior he is expected to exhibit there, and to other events in which the encounter with God is socially organized and prearranged. But the child brings his own God, the one he has himself put together, to this official encounter.[5]

God is liminal, existing "on the boundary between the internal and external worlds."[6] God-image is transitional and helps one make sense of the world (for better or for worse).

God-image is formed from human experiences that are grounded, first and foremost, in infancy. As a child is born, inundated with a new world, their sense of self is rooted and grounded in their mother. In the tender moments when an infant makes eye contact with a mother while feeding, the child sees themselves in the parent. They are mirrored and exist. The parental relationship lays the foundation for a sense of belonging. As the child grows and develops more independence, they begin to learn about trust (or mistrust), the goodness of the world, and how much control they have.[7]

These concepts, outlined by Rizzuto, have been further expanded upon in measurement techniques, which correlate one's sense of self-image to God-image. Based on Rizzuto's theory, "God" can be replaced with "my parent" to develop an understanding of where this God image comes from. The God Image Inventory is built around core questions such as:

- Is God there for me? (Is my parent there for me?)
- Does God want me to grow? (Does my parent want me to grow?)
- Am I good enough for God to love? (Am I good enough for my parents to love?)

5. Rizzuto, *Birth of the Living God*, 7.

6. Lawrence, "Measuring the Image of God," 214; see also Winnicott, "Transitional Objects and Transitional Phenomena," 89–97.

7. Lawrence, "Measuring the Image of God," 215.

- Is God the sort of person who would want to love me? (Is my parent the sort of person who would want to love me?)[8]

James Jones provides a helpful complement to Rizzuto's work by emphasizing relationship. It is not merely how the parent makes the child feel about themselves, but how the child relates to the parent which informs the God-image. Referencing Jones, Jennie Knight notes, "In order to understand a person's image of the divine, we must start by understanding the internalized relationships."[9] A type of transference occurs as relational patterns are projected onto God. It is thus not merely about who God *is* but what relationship one builds with the divine.

Heinz Kohut emphasized that we cannot exist outside of relationship. Our sense of self arises out of being mirrored and idealized by our parents during infancy.[10] As we enter childhood and early adolescence, our perception of others can best be described as twinning. We see others like us, assuming they share the same perspectives, interests, and understandings of the world. This need for mirroring and twinning helps one develop and grow toward a more cohesive sense of self throughout life.[11] The self, however, still seeks a form of idealization that can be found in God.[12] Having a relationship with and seeing oneself in God meets the need for idealization, belonging, and cohesion.[13]

A child's relationship with their parents is spiritually formative.[14] Dickie and colleagues determined that "when children perceived their parents as nurturing and powerful, God too was perceived as nurturing and powerful."[15] The likewise is also true. These perceptions, however, change as children grow and develop into adults. God becomes the "perfect attachment substitute" as children become more independent. The concepts of a powerful mother-God and a nurturing father-God develop in place of the

8. Lawrence, "Measuring the Image of God," 215–16.

9. Knight, *Feminist Mysticism*, 19.

10. Kohut, *Analysis of the Self*, 171; Knight, *Feminist Mysticism*, 21.

11. Randall, "Legacy of Kohut," 109.

12. Strozier, *Heinz Kohut*, 21.

13. Strozier, *Heinz Kohut*, 332; Knight, *Feminist Mysticism*, 21.

14. Birky and Ball, "Parental Trait Influence," 133–37; Gleason, *Growing Up to God*; Tamayo and Desjardins, "Belief Systems and Conceptual Images," 131–40; Vergote, "Concept of God and Parental Images," 79–87; Dickie et al., "Parent-Child Relationships," 25–43.

15. Dickie et al., "Parent-Child Relationships," 31.

ideal parent. Self-perception, grounded in the internalization of these relationships, becomes ever more important to the formation of God-image as one enters early adulthood.

This concept of God-image naturally intersects faith development. James Fowler, heavily influenced by developmental psychologists like Erikson and Piaget, identified six stages of faith that encompass the lifespan of human development.[16] His work sought to "bring understanding to the process by which persons become subjects before and in relation to God and one another."[17] Fowler notes that the primary way we experience selfhood is through our bodies. The body is the reflexive way we come to know the self internally, in response to others and in response to God.[18]

In the Primal stage of faith (birth to two years old) infants emerge into a new environment, and there is no distinction between the self and the mother. In this stage babies learn the fundamentals of safety, trust, and love. As an infant gazes into a mother's eyes, the first sense of identity and belonging is established. As noted in Rizzuto's work, they are mirrored—they exist. In a healthy environment, a child learns within the first two years of life that they are their own being, separate from the mother, but confident in the reality that the mother is a consistent and safe presence. Even if the mother must go away for a short time, she will return. In this stage Fowler identifies a primal faith that exists before language. In correlation with Rizzuto, he notes that concepts of safety, trust, and love are established (or concepts of harm, mistrust, and neglect are established in unhealthy environments).[19]

Fowler's next stage of faith is the Intuitive-Projective Faith. Ranging from ages three to seven, children in this stage begin to make meaning from the world through imagination, symbols, and experiences. According to Fowler, "Experiences of power and powerlessness orient children to a frequently deep existential concern about questions of security, safety, and the power of those upon whom they rely for protection."[20] Intuitive and concrete ideas about good and evil are developed, and the concept of God takes on strong and powerful symbolism. Children are typically drawn to stories where good triumphs over evil, which help them make

16. Fowler, *Faith Development and Pastoral Care.*

17. Fowler, *Faith Development and Pastoral Care*, loc. 580 of 1515.

18. Fowler, *Faith Development and Pastoral Care*, loc. 569 of 1515.

19. Fowler, *Faith Development and Pastoral Care*, loc. 590 of 1515.

20. Fowler, *Faith Development and Pastoral Care*, loc. 611 of 1515.

sense of the world, their own impulses, and their imagination. At this stage of development, children are unable to control their impulses and benefit from healthy parenting that provides guidance, dependable boundaries, and freedom for autonomy and expression.

Fowler's Mythic-Literal stage of faith encapsulates ages seven to twelve. At this stage, children can make distinctions between fantasy and reality. They develop the ability to understand that others have interests and thoughts apart from their own. Here they make meaning by telling stories about themselves, their experiences, and their sense of belonging.[21] Concepts of fairness, moral reciprocity, and justice are strong in this stage of development and provide an "intuitive basis for a construction of God."[22] God concretely rewards those who do good and clearly punishes those who do wrong. This stage, however, lacks self-reflection and the ability to understand the internal motivations of others. In the Mythic-Literal stage, one's own needs, wishes, and interests (or those of others) are not analyzed. They simply exist and drive behavior. Other people are understood through the lens of one's own desires.[23] Here people crave a sense of competence and self-esteem.

The Synthetic-Conventional stage of faith (ranging from age twelve to young adulthood) is characterized by a sense of interpersonal awareness. One's self-image is built on how one thinks others see them. Fowler sums it up well in a couplet: "I see you seeing me; I see the me I think you see."[24]

Internal reflection takes place in conjunction with the mirror that is provided by family and society. There is an effort to create a unified identity as one strings together a metanarrative consisting of their life stories. Value and self-worth are heavily influenced by the affirmation of significant people in one's life like the family. The sense of self is shaped by the roles and relationships one holds. In a healthy system, God is understood as one who knows us intimately, knows who we are becoming, and can be counted on to fulfill a healthy sense of selfhood.[25] It is in this stage that people often develop conformity to an institution or system like the family or church.[26]

21. Fowler, *Faith Development and Pastoral Care*, loc. 644 of 1515.

22. Fowler, *Faith Development and Pastoral Care*, loc. 644 of 1515.

23. Compare this to Kohut's notion of "twinning."

24. Fowler, *Faith Development and Pastoral Care*, loc. 684 of 1515.

25. Fowler, *Faith Development and Pastoral Care*, loc. 689–700 of 1515.

26. Later stages outlined by Fowler (stages 4–6; respectively the individuative reflective faith, conjunctive faith, and universalizing faith) are characterized by a sense of complexity. Individuals take more autonomy and responsibility for what they believe (stage 4), may move beyond traditional religious conventions (stage 5), or even truly embody

## *IMAGO DEI*

While the perception of God is relational, complex, and ever-evolving, theologians consistently note that humanity is made in God's image. What this means, however, has garnered much discussion. Genesis 1:27 states, "God created humankind in his image, in the image of God he created them; male and female he created them." Explanations have encompassed this passage along with other passages from Genesis, Psalms, Ephesians, 2 Corinthians, Romans, Hebrews, and Colossians. Five key themes emerge: the substantive, eschatological, functional, relational, and embodied understandings.[27]

### The Biblical Passages

The term "image" of God is unique to Genesis. It can be found in Gen 1, Gen 5, and Gen 9. Genesis 1:26–31 states:

> Then God said, "Let us make humankind in our image, according to our likeness; and let them have dominion over the fish of the sea, and over the birds of the air, and over the cattle, and over all the wild animals of the earth, and over every creeping thing that creeps upon the earth." So God created humankind in his image, in the image of God he created them; male and female he created them. God blessed them, and God said to them, "Be fruitful and multiply, and fill the earth and subdue it; and have dominion over the fish of the sea and over the birds of the air and over every living thing that moves upon the earth." God said, "See, I have given you every plant yielding seed that is upon the face of all the earth, and every tree with seed in its fruit; you shall have them for food. And to every beast of the earth, and to every bird of the air, and to everything that creeps on the earth, everything that has the breath of life, I have given every green plant for food." And it was so. God

religious teachings and practice (stage 6—rarely achieved).

27. While an exhaustive analysis of the *imago Dei* is far beyond the scope of this work, it is nevertheless imperative to note that each major shift in thought has been informed by the historical context from which it arises. For selective summaries of the historical interpretation of *imago Dei*, see the following: Simango, "Imago Dei"; Clines, "Image of God in Man," 54–61; Miller, "In the Image and Likeness of God"; Hoekema, *Created in God's Image*, 33–65; Westermann, *Genesis 1–11*, 148–58. A more comprehensive summary of the historical development of the *imago Dei* can be found in Jonsson, *Image of God*.

> saw everything that he had made, and indeed, it was very good.
> And there was evening and there was morning, the sixth day.

Genesis 5 and Gen 9 support it. Genesis 5 contains the genealogy of Adam, and at the outset it states, "When God created humankind, he made them in the likeness of God" (Gen 5:1). Later in Gen 9:6, God gives instructions to Noah and says, "Whoever sheds the blood of a human, by a human shall that person's blood be shed; for in his own image God made humankind." Each of these passages, in turn, highlight the privileged nature of humanity. Humanity shares its nature with both animals and God. Francisco notes this by saying that humanity was "created on the same day that the higher animals were formed . . . but also possesses the image of God."[28] Brueggemann goes on to note that "the image of God in the human person is a mandate or power and responsibility."[29] Humanity, then, is "to be God as God would be to the nonhuman, to be an extension of God's own dominion."[30]

While Genesis alone refers to the "image" of God, other biblical passages, such as Ps 8:3–8, have a similar language that points to the privileged state of humanity:

> When I look at your heavens, the work of your fingers,
> the moon and the stars that you have established;
> *what are human beings that you are mindful of them,*
> *mortals that you care for them?*
> *Yet you have made them a little lower than God,*
> *and crowned them with glory and honor.*
> *You have given them dominion over the works of your hands;*
> *you have put all things under their feet,*
> all sheep and oxen,
> and also the beasts of the field,
> the birds of the air, and the fish of the sea,
> whatever passes along the paths of the seas.[31]

The psalmist notes that humanity has been tasked with the care for creation while simultaneously showing God's care for human beings. "Crowned with glory and honor," humanity is set apart from the rest of creation as caretakers and co-creators of the world. Repeatedly, throughout the biblical

28. Francisco, "Genesis Commentary," 125.
29. Brueggemann, *Genesis*, 32.
30. Fretheim, *New Interpreter's Bible*, 345.
31. Emphasis added.

text, God is named as Creator. Humanity, in God's image, is also given the ability to create and shape the surrounding world. Unlike animals that are driven by mere instinct, humanity can reason and effect change for better or worse.[32]

Several New Testament epistles allude to the image of God, albeit in a decidedly different way than Genesis. Ephesians notes that in Christ humanity is encouraged to "put on the new self, created after the likeness of God in true righteousness and holiness" (Eph 4:23–24). Second Corinthians proclaims that Christ is the image of God"[33] and that when human beings behold the "glory of the Lord [they are] transformed into the same image" (2 Cor 3:18). Romans 8 describes being "conformed to the image of His Son" (Rom 8:29). Each of these passages notes a transformation to become more like Jesus as the old way of life is shed.[34]

Jesus is understood in New Testament texts as made in God's image. Porteous calls him the "perfect reflection" of *imago Dei* set forth in Genesis.[35] This is evidenced in Hebrews as the author ascribes to Jesus the psalmist's description of humanity:

> What are human beings that you are mindful of them, or mortals, that you care for them? You have made them for a little while lower than the angels; you have crowned them with glory and honor, subjecting all things under their feet.
>
> Now in subjecting all things to them, God left nothing outside their control. As it is, we do not yet see everything in subjection to them, *but we do see Jesus*, who for a little while was made lower than the angels, *now crowned with glory and honor* because of the suffering of death, so that by the grace of God he might taste death for everyone.[36] (Heb 2:6–9)

Jesus often refers to himself as the Son of Man. Second Corinthians 4:4 and Col 1:5 identify Jesus as the ideal prototype of the *imago Dei*. Colossians states:

32. Francisco, "Genesis Commentary," 125.

33. 2 Cor 4:4: "In their case the god of this world has blinded the minds of unbelievers, to keep them from seeing the light of the gospel of the glory of Christ, who is the image of God."

34. Barr, "Image of God and Natural Theology."

35. Grenz, "Jesus as the Imago Dei," 619.

36. Emphasis added; compare to emphasis in Ps 8.

> [Jesus] is the image of the invisible God, the firstborn of all creation; for in him all things in heaven and on earth were created, things visible and invisible, whether thrones or dominions or rulers or powers—all things have been created through him and for him. He himself is before all things, and in him all things hold together. He is the head of the body, the church; he is the beginning, the firstborn from the dead, so that he might come to have first place in everything. For in him all the fullness of God was pleased to dwell, and through him God was pleased to reconcile to himself all things, whether on earth or in heaven, by making peace through the blood of his cross. (Col 1:15–20)

The word used for likeness or image, Grenz notes, is *eikōn*. "*Eikōn* carries the force of 'what completely corresponds to the "prototype" or the "perfect reflection of the prototype."'" He goes on to state that *eikōn* further means that one actively participates in the reality depicted. Therefore, Jesus actively embodies the ideal form of *imago Dei*.[37]

## The Substantive Understanding

As Christian thought developed, theologians debated the nature of Jesus's humanity and divinity. Simultaneously, Gnostic thought developed, which sought to understand the relationship between body and spirit.[38] How divine was Jesus? How human was Jesus? In Gnostic thought, the material world, including the body, was deemed corrupt and the spiritual world was deemed good as the divinity of Jesus was elevated. The *imago Dei* became understood substantively—there is a shared substance between God and humanity. In other words, the *imago Dei* is something that humanity possesses.

Irenaeus (ca. 120–203 CE) posited that humanity is modeled after the image and likeness of Jesus or God the Son.[39] In his writings he noted, "Now God shall be glorified in His handiwork, fitting it so as to be conformable to, and modeled after, His own Son. For by the hands of the Father, that is by the Son and the Holy Spirit, man, and not [merely] a part of man, was

37. Ridderbos, *Paul*, 70–76; for a more detailed and nuanced discussion outlining this argument refer to the following texts: Grenz, "Jesus as the Imago Dei"; Dunn, *Epistles to the Colossians*; Lightfoot, *Saint Paul's Epistles*.

38. Morris, *Revival of the Gnostic Heresy*, ch. 1, "Influences of Gnosticism"; Pearson, "Early Christianity and Gnosticism," 81–106; Brakke, *Gnostics*, ch. 4, "Imagining Gnosticism."

39. Weinandy, "St. Irenaeus and the *Imago Dei*," 19.

made in the likeness of God."[40] For Irenaeus, the body is made in God's image (as noted when God the Son, Jesus, became human) but humanity must grow into the likeness of God. By embracing the *imago Dei* one spiritually matures, grows in relationship with God, and is transformed into a moral and faithful being.[41] This growth and maturity are made possible by the Holy Spirit and modeled by Jesus, thus making Irenaeus's understanding of *imago Dei* deeply Trinitarian. The body is celebrated as humanity comes to understand the *imago Dei*. It is not evil or corrupt as Gnosticism taught, but it is a remarkable and significant expression of God, idealized through Jesus. Thomas Weinandy states it well:

> Irenaeus delighted in the unparalleled and literally incredible thought that human beings, in the totality of who we are, body and soul, are images of God, and were created so by God himself. . . . For Irenaeus, to be simply human clothes us with a dignity that is inconceivable, a dignity that pertains not to some spiritual aspect of our being, but to our very created humanness. It is the very humanness of human beings that, for Irenaeus, reflects who and what God is, for in making us human he made us in his own likeness.[42]

Approximately two hundred years later, Augustine (354–430 CE) offered his reflection on the *imago Dei*. For Augustine, the image of God in humanity was both spiritual and rational. Unlike Irenaeus, he did not differentiate between the image and likeness of God. Instead, he understood the *imago Dei* as a human trinity of memory, understanding, and love. In other words, the *imago Dei* points to the human capacity to remember, know, and love God. He posited that the *imago Dei* was corrupted during the fall (Gen 3) but that God offers redemption through Jesus. Remembering, knowing, and loving Jesus brings renewed knowledge of God and thus the restoration of the *imago Dei*.[43] He states:

> The mind must first be considered as it is in itself before it becomes a partaker of God, and His image must be found in it. For, as we have said, although worn out and defaced by losing participation of God, yet the image still remains. For it is His image, in this very

40. Irenaeus, *Against Heresies* 5.6.1.

41. Weinandy, "St. Irenaeus and the *Imago Dei*," 22–23; Barr, "Image of God and Natural Theology."

42. Weinandy, "St. Irenaeus and the *Imago Dei*," 17.

43. Augustine, *On the Holy Trinity*, 142; Simango, "Imago Dei," 2; Barr, "Image of God and Natural Theology."

> point, that it is capable of Him; which so great good is only possible by its being His image.[44]

Augustine was very much informed by Neoplatonic thought. Similar to Plato's understanding of forms, Augustine believed that God is the perfect form of truth and goodness.[45] His doctrine of original sin posits that evil is a corruption of the good. Humanity, made in God's image, was created with free will and therefore had the capacity to sin. The fall that occurs in Gen 3 causes humanity to become enslaved to sin. This original sin, Augustine believed, was transmitted to subsequent generations through sexual lust and desire.[46] From our conception, then, humanity is complicit in the original sin of Genesis. Restoration of the *imago Dei* is made possible through the pursuit of God. This pursuit of God is a spiritual and rational endeavor that links memory, understanding, and love through Jesus.

Thomas Aquinas (1225–74 CE), informed by the rise of monasticism and scholarship in thirteenth-century Christianity, found reason to be the predominant way to know and understand God.[47] Like Irenaeus, Aquinas distinguished between the image and likeness of God and, like Augustine, he believed the image of God pointed to humanity's ability to reason. He notes that "man possesses a natural aptitude for understanding and loving God and this aptitude consists in the very nature of the mind, which is common to all men."[48] Aquinas argued that the likeness of God is moral in nature. Through sin and the fall, humanity has become immoral and fallen away from the likeness of God. This likeness is restored through the supernatural grace of God. "Man," Aquinas notes, "habitually knows and loves God, though imperfectly. This image consists in the conformity of grace."[49]

Man has been given rationality and dominion over creation. Aquinas goes on to note that "man knows and loves God perfectly and this image consists in the likeness of glory." Woman, made from man, does not possess this quality.[50] Man, however, is made in the image of God in three ways: creation (intellect), re-creation (grace), and likeness (dominion). According

44. Augustine, *On the Holy Trinity*, 189.

45. Mattox, "Augustine"; Kung, *Great Christian Thinkers*, 69–98; Brown, *Augustine of Hippo*.

46. Vorster, "Calvin's Modification," 79.

47. Wei, *Intellectual Culture in Medieval Paris*; Pasnau, "Saint Thomas Aquinas."

48. Thomas Aquinas, *Summa Theologica* (ed. Hutchins), 495–96.

49. Thomas Aquinas, *Summa Theologica* (ed. Hutchins), 495–96.

50. Thomas Aquinas, *Summa Theologica* I q.93. art.4.

to Aquinas, "The first is found in all men, the second only in the just, and third only in the blessed." Like Irenaeus, he taught that the likeness of God could be restored through Christ. The image of God, however, remains in the rational faculty of humanity.[51]

Irenaeus, Augustine, and Aquinas all understood the *imago Dei* substantively via intellect and reason. Influenced by Greek philosophy and the New Testament, they each, in their own way, emphasized humanity's ability to know God. Irenaeus emphasized the ability to grow and mature into a moral being while celebrating both materiality and the spirit. Augustine focused on the trinity of memory, understanding, and love to find redemption and restore the fallen *imago Dei.* Aquinas taught that the *imago Dei* is humanity's ability to reason. They all taught that something (be it image or likeness) was damaged during the fall and that restoration was possible via Christ.

## The Eschatological Understanding

During the Reformation, theologians such as Martin Luther (1483–1546) and John Calvin (1509–64) developed distinctly eschatological understandings of the *imago Dei.* Luther rejected the distinction between the image and likeness of God but understood the *imago Dei* as both public and private. He used the public image of *imago Dei* to refer to humankind's intelligence and will, which were preserved after the fall. The private image of righteousness, however, was lost. This private *imago Dei* is modeled after the corrupt Adam who was led astray by the Devil. Thus, fallen humanity is seen in the image of the Devil. Luther states that:

> God willed that man should sigh after the restoration of that "image of God" which he had lost; and should therefore the more hate sin, which had been the cause of this awful calamity; and that Adam should admonish his posterity of what had been the consequence of his sin; that when, having been plundered of his reason by Satan, he thought he should become like God, he became like Satan himself.[52]

51. Thomas Aquinas, *Summa Theologica* (ed. Hutchins), 493–96 (I q.93. art.4); Hoekema, *Created in God's Image*, 33–35; Barr, "Image of God"; Simango, "Imago Dei," 175–76.

52. Luther, *Luther on Creation*, 22.

Christ, however, can restore this brokenness. The corrupted image of humanity will be restored in the last days.[53]

For Calvin, sin and the fall in Gen 3 destroyed the image of God in humanity and alienated humanity from God. Although the *imago Dei* is not totally annihilated, what remains is a "frightful deformity."[54] Calvin goes on to note that redemption is only possible in the elect that have been born in the Spirit. For these few, true restoration will be possible when they enter heaven.[55]

Luther and Calvin, products of the Reformation, have a notably more sinister understanding of how sin harms the reality of *imago Dei*. Redemption is far off and obtainable during the last days (Luther) or only for the elect when they enter heaven (Calvin). These Reformation thinkers also move away from a distinction between the image and likeness of God. The *imago Dei* is centered in the soul or spirit of humanity rather than in one's intellect and reason.

## The Functional Understanding

A turn to a more spiritual and psychological understanding of *imago Dei* occurred in the 1800s with thinkers such as August Dillmann (1823–94), Carl Friedrich Keil (1807–88), and Franz Delitzsch (1813–90). Contemporaries to Sigmund Freud, the birth of psychology led scholars to consider how one's behavior displays the *imago Dei*. These thinkers, as well as feminist thinkers, also considered the functional impact of how one's understanding of the *imago Dei* affected their human and societal behavior.

Dillmann understood *imago Dei* as a combination of humankind's physical form and mental capacities. This included free will, self-consciousness, and the capacity of thought for what is true and good. The physical and intellectual, he argued, are not separate or different from the spirit. Rather, they combine to give robust meaning to the concept of *imago Dei*.

53. Simango, "Imago Dei," 177–78. It is no doubt that Luther's understanding of *imago Dei* was shaped by his experience within the church. The sale of indulgences, corruption of priests, and immorality that he saw in Christendom likely influenced the darker understanding of a fallen *imago Dei* that he presented. See the following for more information: Luther, *Luther's Works*, 1:65; see also Cairns, *Image of God in Man*, 124; Althaus, *Theology of Martin Luther*, 158; Hendrix, "Luther"; McCue, "'Simul iustus et peccator,'" 81–96; Grimm, "Luther's Inner Conflict," 173–86.

54. Simango, "Imago Dei," 177–78.

55. Calvin, *Institutes*, 186; Simango, "Imago Dei," 177–78.

The "moral religious perfection" that was harmed during the fall can be restored through Christ.[56] Similarly, Keil and Delitzsch argued for a "spiritual personality of man" that displayed the *imago Dei* through actions and behaviors in the world. This understanding combined mind, spirit, and physical body.[57] It is the human capacity for goodness, dominion, growth, and restoration.

Feminist scholars are also concerned with functional and metacognitive understanding and reflect deeply on how the teaching itself influences society. Scholars such as Mary Daly, Elisabeth Schüssler Fiorenza, Rosemary Radford Ruether, and Hye Kyung Heo have noted that God's image is often described in masculine terms.[58] The andro-centrism of the *imago Dei*, then, is inherent and has a significant detrimental impact upon women. Mary Daly is most well known for stating, "If God is male, male is God."[59] The subjugation and dehumanization of women is made possible, in part, by the tendency for society to elevate the masculine and deem the feminine as less than. In other words, God has predominantly been thought of as male so women have not been seen as image-bearers of God. Hye Kyung Heo notes the importance of instilling feminine language into conversations about God as feminine imagery orients society toward gender equality. She states, "Because God is named Father, Son, and Spirit the Trinity has been regarded as contributing to the conception of a male God. Undeniably it has been used to legitimize patriarchy and justify the subordination of women to men."[60] This concept of utilizing feminine language for God and its implications has been richly reflected upon among feminist scholars.

In light of androcentrism and the patriarchal language used for God, feminist scholars advocate for a new language for God. The way one talks about God influences how God-image and how humanity understands God acting in the world. These power dynamics are significant in addressing issues of oppression and dehumanization. One such example of this reimagined language can be found in the work of Elisabeth Schüssler Fiorenza

56. Simango, "Imago Dei," 177–78; Dillmann, *Genesis*, 80. Also cited in Jonsson, *Image of God*, 82.

57. Keil and Delitzsch, *Commentary on the Old Testament*, 63–64; Simango, "Imago Dei," 178–79.

58. See, for example, Daly, *Beyond God the Father*; Daly, *Church and the Second Sex*; Radford Ruether, *Sexism and God Talk*; Schüssler Fiorenza, *But She Said*; Schüssler Fiorenza, *In Memory of Her*; Schüssler Fiorenza, *Wisdom Ways*; Heo, *Liberative Cross*.

59. Daly, *Beyond God the Father*, 19.

60. Heo, *Liberative Cross*, 48.

and Rosemary Radford Ruether. They explore God-language through a discussion on the divine goddess Sophia or Wisdom. Sophia instills feminine language into God and curates peace for all humankind. This feminine understanding of Sophia can be found throughout Christian history despite the dominant expressions of a male Logos. According to Ruether, "The figure of the Holy Spirit picks up many of the Hebraic traditions of the female Sophia . . . [and] many early Christian texts refer to the Spirit as female."[61] It is this deep Wisdom, manifest as femininity in the biblical text, that moves society to a deeper appreciation for the feminine.

Another example can be found in Dorothee Sölle. In her work, she challenges the "father" language and culture of obedience that surrounds God-image. She asks, "why do people revere a God whose most important quality is power, whose interest is in subduing, who fears equality, a being who is addressed as Lord, for whom mere power is not enough, so that his theologians have to credit him with omnipotence?"[62] She notes that she does not wish to make power the focal point of her life. While the symbol "male" and "father" is associated with dominance and authority, Jesus is relatable for the opposite reasons. He has an identity as the "powerless Christ who was independent of authority, who has nothing but his love with which to win and save us."[63] Sölle notes that using father language is one way to talk about God. It is, however, limiting, and she advocates for a theological language "free of dominance."[64]

Many of these feminist reflections draw upon Moltmann's understanding of the Social Trinitarian model. Moltmann's model incorporates three persons-in-one, preserving both unity and diversity. It is not hierarchical but rather communal. It is in this space of relationship that feminist scholars like Elizabeth Johnson and Heo situate their theological reflection. The Trinity has feminine aspects and so women are image bearers of God. When women are thought of as image bearers of God, it works to destabilize oppressive structures of abuse and dominance perpetuated by androcentrism.[65]

61. Radford Ruether, *Sexism and God Talk*, 58–59.

62. Sölle, "Fatherhood, Power, and Barbarism," 330.

63. Sölle, "Fatherhood, Power, and Barbarism," 330.

64. Sölle, "Fatherhood, Power, and Barbarism," 331.

65. Moder, "Women, Personhood, and the Male God," 85–103.

## The Relational Understanding

The writings of Karl Barth and Emil Brunner, developed around World War I and World War II, advocate for a more relational understanding of *imago Dei*. As humanity was torn apart by war and dehumanization, Barth and Brunner marked another important shift in understanding. It is in the intersection of relationship that the potential of the *imago Dei* manifests.

Barth understood the *imago Dei* as the capacity for relationship. Although his exegetical work has been criticized, Barth understood the sentence "male and female he created them" to describe the preceding sentence, "in the image of God he created them." He argued that humanity has, since its very beginnings, existed in relationship to one another and to God. This image of God is made fully known through Jesus. Barth says, "The humanity of Jesus is not merely the repetition and reflection of His divinity, or of God's controlling will; it is the repetition and reflection of God Himself, no more and no less. It is the image of God, the *imago Dei*."[66] Humanity's relationship with God has been destroyed during the fall, but it is through a Trinitarian and Christocentric approach that redemption is made possible.[67]

Brunner, in dialogue with Barth, noted that *imago Dei* is not something that humanity possesses. It is not a spiritual, physical, intellectual, or moral descriptor. Rather, *imago Dei* is the point of contact between humanity and God. While Brunner agreed with Barth that the *imago Dei* was destroyed during the fall, his understanding of the point of contact made restoration possible. Like others before him, Brunner argued that the functional aspects of *imago Dei* remained (dominion, materiality, etc.), while the moral concept was diminished via sin. Despite this, *imago Dei*, even in a sinful humanity, "functioned as a 'point of contact.'"[68]

James Barr, examining the dialogue between Barth and Brunner, argued that reflecting upon the *imago Dei* illuminates God more so than humanity. The *imago Dei*, he noted, was not something to be possessed or an internal quality. It is rather a point of contact that opens humanity to a rich analogy that encompasses numerous aspects of identity and creation. Historically, reflection upon the *imago Dei* sought to deduce what it *is*. Barr

66. Barth, *Church Dogmatics*, 3/2:219.

67. Barth, *Church Dogmatics*, 3/2:324–25; Barr, "Image of God and Natural Theology"; also cited in Simango, "Imago Dei," 180.

68. Barr, "Image of God and Natural Theology," 161.

and others focus instead on functional and analogical aspects of the teaching. He states, "If the image of God is relevant for discussion at all, it must mean much more than a tiny 'point of contact,' it must mean something like a deep and wide interface containing and providing numerous aspects of community or analogy."[69] In other words, for Barr, an analogical understanding of the *imago Dei* creates space for rich reflection on identity and creation, prompting individuals and communities to care for creation accordingly.

## The Embodied Understanding

Each of the frameworks employed to understand *imago Dei* are embodied. The mind and intellect, relationships and personal growth, morality, and engagement with the world are all filtered through, shaped by, and experienced by the body. It is thus ultimately through the body that one comes to know what it means to be made in God's image.

For Christians, Jesus is the ideal manifestation of *imago Dei.* His divinity, humanity, relationships, and actions exemplify the ideal life. The life of Jesus introduced a new incarnational understanding of God. Elisabeth Moltmann-Wendel notes that "the beginnings of the Jesus movement are stamped by a revaluation of the body."[70] In the act of becoming human God is made flesh and thus experiences life alongside humanity. It is through this embodied experience that Jesus encounters ordinary human experiences—he feels frustration, pain, joy, and love.[71]

Medieval female mystics embraced the embodiment of Christ in powerful ways. Embracing their spirituality in a patriarchal culture that devalued the body, female mystics took a different approach. They often identified "more deeply with their socially marginalized bodies, sinking into their own physicality and mortality rather than attempting to transcend it."[72] In doing so they discovered profound joy and love in the passion narratives and "declared the redemptive power of their own bodies."[73] The imitation of Christ was written on the bodies of mystics as they sought

69. Barr, "Image of God and Natural Theology," 171.

70. Moltmann-Wendel, *I Am My Body*, 36.

71. The embodied experience of Jesus will be explored in much greater detail in subsequent chapters.

72. Esposito, "Embodying Mysticism," 4–5.

73. Esposito, "Embodying Mysticism," 5.

a path of tribulation. Angela of Foligno, for example, "writes her body" as she communicates her bodily gestures and visions. Her body endured weariness and pain as she came to know the suffering Christ. She is well known for intense penitential practices and her visions of drinking from the wound on Christ's side.[74]

There is much debate regarding the empowerment or subjugation of women in these embodied acts. However, scholars contend that these spiritual expressions provided a bodily understanding of God in a way that predominantly rational spiritualities of the time did not. Contemporary embodied theologians find insight in this spiritual expression and contend that the body is revelatory of God. Emphasizing sexuality, social location, and experience, the body is seen as both a site and sign of religious truth.

## DEICIDE: THE DEATH OF HOW WE KNOW GOD

So, who *is* God and what does it mean to be made in God's image? The answer is muddied for those who have endured incest. Harm goes far beyond the body and psyche. It is spiritual, impacting the very notion of who God is and how one comes to know God. The familial relationship informs one's personal and intimate understanding of self and God. For survivors of incest, the familial relationship is fraught with mistrust, instability, fear, and violation. One's self-image becomes riddled with shame, guilt, and self-loathing as violation becomes encoded into the flesh. Truly identifying with the concept of *imago Dei* is problematic at multiple levels, making incest an oppressive and compounded harm that results in a death of how one comes to know God.

Psychoanalytic theorists have postulated that one's God-image is formed through a dynamic process of internalized relationships that grow and evolve over time. We seek belonging, understanding, and idealization as we come to know ourselves and the world. We also encounter myths, symbols, and religious teachings as we age and develop. Experiences of power and powerlessness, good and evil, right and wrong, and justice and injustice mold our understandings, and our identities become wrapped up in how we think others perceive us.

The family system is not healthy for those who have experienced incest. It is characterized by dysfunction, bodily violation, harm, and fear. During infancy, it is likely that the child is not granted the opportunity

74. Elliott, "Flesh and Spirit," 27.

to experience a truly safe, connective, and nurturing environment. If a consistent sense of belonging, trust, and safety is not mirrored when the child gazes into their caretakers' eyes, then the foundation for developing a healthy self-image and the Primal stage of faith is disrupted.

In dysfunctional family systems children often carry the weight of holding the family together.[75] They are dehumanized and exploited, and their pain is invisible as they find themselves caught up in the tornado of someone else's pain. Fear, loss of control, silence, oppression, and violation characterize daily reality. Feelings about parental figures may be complicated. They seek love, protection, and belonging, and while they may not receive it from caregivers, they often freely give it. Feelings of powerlessness consume the Intuitive-Projective stage of faith as children learn that this harm is ordinary. This painful relational pattern becomes projected onto God alongside the idealized hopes of love.

Although the age ranges Fowler associates with each stage of faith are merely suggestive, most abuse of girls occurs between the Mythic-Literal and the Synthetic-Conventional stages. The powerfully symbolic God with a strong sense of justice does not intervene. The expectation of immediate salvation from harm is met with the reality of ongoing abuse. One's identity takes on the expectations placed upon them by the family. Often this means children feel responsible for holding dysfunctional family dynamics together. Maintaining silence, enduring abuse, and embodying the dehumanization associated with such abuse continue to shape one's sense of self and God.

The body becomes an inescapable crime scene, bloodied with the ashes of one's innocence. Memory becomes encoded into the flesh as flashbacks, intrusive memories, hypervigilance, and fear become an ordinary part of life. At some point, the creative and carefree child, tasked with co-creating God's world by embarking upon their wildest dreams and imaginations, is shattered. The sexually abused child learns that she is not a person before God. In repeated instances of abuse, she learns that God is not there for her, that she is not worthy of love and protection, and that she has no control over her own body. In the sexually abused body of a child, the *imago Dei* is very much at risk.

Augustine reminds us that the *imago Dei* points to the body's capacity to remember, know, and love God. Substantive approaches note that the *imago Dei* is something that human beings possess. Augustinian and

75. Pelletier and Handy, "Is Family Dysfunction More Harmful," 53–54.

Thomistic reflections highlight the intellect and the human ability for rational thought. It is our capacity to know God that makes us in God's image. For those who have experienced incest, however, this substantive understanding is disrupted. When brought into dialogue with psychoanalytic understandings, it is apparent that the very ability to know who God is becomes muddied by painful formative experiences. The bodily, psychological, and social pain endured mutates this rational capacity. While one may intellectually know who God is, true *knowing* in the depths of one's innermost being is dealt a fatal wound.

Eschatological understandings of *imago Dei* emphasize restoration for the elect in the last days. It is something we grow toward in life. This promise of restoration for the worthy is often inaccessible to those living with the enduring reality of incest. The impact of such harm permeates all aspects of life long after the events themselves have ended. Personal growth must take a long and arduous path while navigating a trauma-saturated body. Suicide, addiction, cancer, autoimmune disorder, cardiovascular diseases, anxiety, depression, and a myriad of other illnesses become companions on the journey. With a painful relationship with God already permeating one's understanding, the promise of a far-off redemption resulting from personal growth seems impossible and patronizing. Yet again, the *imago Dei* is wounded.

The *imago Dei* fares hardly better if understood relationally. Barth and Brunner envisioned it as a point of contact between both one another and the divine. As noted, however, relationships are particularly painful for those who have experienced incest. Not only are the family system and God image disruptive, but the far-reaching effects of this violence often color interpersonal relationships as well. High rates of promiscuity, borderline personality disorder, addiction, and mood disorders are prevalent, making this "point of contact" messy.

The *imago Dei* is understood through human behavior in Functionalist approaches. Not only is it the human capacity for good, but it also points to how the concept itself shapes engagement with the world. Is it liberative, inclusive, and restorative? Psychologists and feminist theologians aim for a more holistic understanding of the God image. How can the concept of *imago Dei* liberate, include, and restore those who have experienced incest?

In truth, the *imago Dei* can be understood through all these perspectives. It points to something that humans possess, actions and behaviors, the capacity for relationship, and an ideal to grow toward. In its purest form, it is the innate and bodily way in which humanity remembers, knows, and loves God throughout life. It is liberative, restorative, and embodied. It surpasses the limits of language to help us know ourselves as God knows us. Mystics and embodied theologians alike articulated this knowing through the body.

How one comes to know the self and God is shaped by the bodily experience of incest. One's God-image is layered with harm, disappointment, and unmet expectations. The body becomes a place of intolerable touch. The flesh crawls, alive and teeming with inescapable memory. As Grovijahn puts it, "For a young girl victimized by another's brutalizing touch, more than just her flesh is violated. Her very self—that root of whatever we like to think makes us persons—is attacked and violated. And somewhere in that place or location of raped subjectivity, God is very much at risk."[76] This deicide, or death of how we know God, is overwhelming. It can leave one gasping for breath, staring emptily into the abyss, desperate for confirmation from God. It is often met with resounding silence as the body cycles between episodes of dissociation and intolerable flashbacks.

It is not sufficient to merely say that the experience of incest alters one's perception of God. This harm strikes a fatal wound into one's identity, shaping how one comes to know self, God, and the world. This gashing wound of deicide is felt within the body, and one must learn to inhabit this space. It is by locating God in the most painful and taboo reaches of one's experience that a new way of knowing can occur. The sexually abused body is a space of both deicide and resurrection. It is within this body that God is revealed.

76. Grovijahn, "Theology as an Irruption into Embodiment," 32.

## 3

# Embodiment

*My Body Knows*
*the fear of darkness, the touch of shame, the pain of penetration.*
*The silent, compliant, disempowerment.*
*The grit won from endurance and escape.*
*The intoxicating frenzy of stillness.*
*My Body Knows*
*How to protect, how to remember, how to survive.*

*Maybe somehow my body can forget.*
*I fled. I flourished. I married. I divorced.*
*I lost myself. I found myself. I got high. I got sober. I found love.*

*My body still remembers*
*The invisible hands*
*My arms pinned to my sides*
*The stench of stale Camel cigarettes*
*The sloppy kiss*
*The caress on the back of my elbow.*

*My Body Knows*
*I am not safe.*
*I cannot escape my own flesh.*

*And yet . . .*
*My body is born of the cosmos*
*Relentlessly pursuing divinity.*
*The violation of my body will be the revelation of my truth.*

To be human is to be embodied. All human experiences are known, first and foremost, through the body. At birth, our bodies enter the world to discover new sights, sounds, and smells. Through life we live, learn, and mature in ever-changing and dynamic bodies. It is through our bodies that we experience love, sadness, joy, and pain. It is through our bodies that we know God and discover ourselves as made in God's image.

For those who have experienced incest, bodily knowing can be particularly difficult. Because such harm and violation occur within the body, learning to inhabit and tolerate the body is challenging. Escaping the body is often a necessary and efficient survival tool during abuse. In the aftermath, however, this defense mechanism keeps one from living a full life. Dissociation is common, and many resort to self-medicating to ease the pain of inhabiting a sexually violated body that continually relives the abuse. This contributes to the death of how one knows God.

Scientific and religious thinkers agree, however, that the body holds wisdom that the conscious mind does not. It is in this embodied space that a new way of knowing God can be discovered. The location of the sexually abused body, so readily dehumanized, degraded, and discredited, is a space of profound knowledge and truth. Despite the harm done, the sexually violated body is revelatory of God.

## SOCIAL LOCATION

The human body, in all its varying forms, carries social truth and divine revelation in its flesh. It is imbued with a complexity that reflects how the body engages both God and the world. Crossan notes that it can function as a "microcosm for the macrocosm of political society."[1] In other words, the way in which one's body is encountered in society is reflective of larger social understandings of the world.[2] The sexually abused body of a child, then, carries a social location that is both oppressive and revelatory.

1. Crossan, *Jesus*, 76.

2. Douglas, *Purity and Danger*, 115; Douglas, *Natural Symbols*, xiv; Crossan, *Jesus*, 77.

In the Synoptic Gospels, the story of the hemorrhaging woman offers a helpful parallel.[3] The woman bleeds for twelve years and she suffers physically, financially, and socially. She has spent all that she has on doctors and is unable to find a cure. Her condition, according to Jewish purity laws, means that she is unclean and therefore socially isolated.[4] She would not be able to have ordinary social contact with family (including her husband if she were married) and she would not be permitted to engage in any religious activities. A profound loneliness permeates her story.[5] Her suffering led her to abandon customs and seek Jesus out in a crowd. Doing so was a violation of ritual purity law, which placed others in the crowd (including Jesus) in a state of uncleanness.[6]

Jesus heals the woman as he does so many others considered unclean or cast out by society.[7] She tells him her whole story and, in response, he calls her "daughter" and tells her that her faith has made her well and to go in peace. It would be easy to imagine this story going a different way. Her uncleanness and bold violation of the law could just as easily have resulted in her demise. Jesus or the crowd could have turned on her. Instead, she finds healing as Jesus restores both a sense of belonging and bodily wholeness.[8]

For those who have experienced incest, the body resides in this state of social isolation. Much like the woman's issue of blood, the impurity may not be visible to the naked eye, but it is nevertheless embodied. Many report feeling "dirty" or "ashamed," feelings that are directly connected to the bodily experiences of incest. Often victims of incest will search for relief through avenues that numb the experience. The gospel healing invites us to reevaluate the body. In this case, "healing" does not result in the years of pain being erased (as so many survivors wish). Instead, it is socially, relationally, and spiritually restorative. It creates space for a previously "unclean" body to know belonging and love.

3. This story can be found in Mark 5:25–34, Matt 9:20–22, and Luke 8:43–48.

4. See Lev 15:19–31.

5. Getty-Sullivan, *Women in the New Testament*, 64.

6. Collins, "Purity," 725.

7. For example, the healing of the leper (Mark 1:40–45) and the story of the good Samaritan (Luke 10:25–37); see Greenfield, *Subversive Jesus*; McKinney Fox, *Disability and the Way of Jesus.*

8. Moltmann-Wendel, *I Am My Body*, 37.

The whole story of those who have experienced incest, however, carries with it a decidedly *dis*embodied history. Christian thought has worked hard to mark bodies, particularly female bodies, with a shameful social location. Early Christian thought viewed the world dualistically. Platonism emphasized a world of perfect forms alongside a deceptive material world that imprisoned the soul in bodily imperfections.[9] Combined with Stoic thought, which emphasized control over senses and passions, the soul came to be viewed as greater than the body.[10] The sinful flesh became something to overcome. Control of the body helped one serve God's will. This dualistic understanding marked the body with shame.

Throughout Christian history, men have enjoyed a dominant social position. The church fathers established early on that men, stewards of reason, were in a superior position to know God. Women, meanwhile, were associated with the body, sensuality, and sin.[11] This was prefaced and underlined by significant theologians in the church. Tertullian went as far as to say to women:

> *You* are the devil's gateway: *you* are the unsealer of that (forbidden) tree: *you* are the first deserter of the divine law: *you* are she who persuaded him whom the devil was not valiant enough to attack. *You* destroyed so easily God's image, man. On account of *your* desert—that is, death—even the Son of God had to die.[12]

And Jerome is noted for saying:

> As long as the woman lives for birth and children, there is the same difference between her and the male as that between body and soul. But if she wants to serve Christ more than the world, she will cease to be woman and will be called man, because we want all the perfect to be exalted to become man.[13]

Augustine stated, "That home is good in which man commands and the woman obeys. That person is good in whom the spirit rules and the flesh serves."[14] The undisciplined body (and particularly the female body) was

9. Blumenthal and Armstrong, "Platonism."

10. Rasimus et al., *Stoicism in Early Christianity.*

11. Allen, *Concept of Woman*, 176–78; Beonio-Brocchieri, "Feminine Mind," 29–30.

12. Tertullian, "On the Apparel of Women" 1.1.

13. Moltmann-Wendel, *I Am My Body*, 43; Jerome, *Commentariorum in Epistolam ad Ephesios*, 533.

14. Moltmann-Wendel, *I Am My Body*, 43; Augustine, *De Trinitate*, col 205.

viewed as leading one away from the spiritual life. Ordinary functions of the body such as desire, sexuality, and childbirth corrupt one's spiritual life.

Augustine notes that in sexual desire, men experience bodily arousal "which is not (as it would have been in paradise) under the control of his mind."[15] The penalty of the fall, then, is that "the masculine is subjugated to the inferior feminine," to sensual desire.[16] Sexuality was an interior state to be conquered, and even in marriage it could draw one away from God.[17] He posited that it was the woman's responsibility to veil herself and not "stimulate" men.[18] Augustine's language surrounding the body and women has a significant and lasting influence on Christianity. His justifications and understandings of sexuality and sin lay the groundwork for victim blaming.

Reason, and therefore masculinity, became the dominant way to know God as the church established and supported the rise of universities. Man's position of a superior and rational spiritual life became further solidified. Well into the Middle Ages, Thomas Aquinas noted that a human being is made up of both body and soul. The soul is rational, informs the material body, and operates as an organizing principle for the body.[19] Intellect, then, is the highest expression of humanity. Thomistic thought understands the body through its unification with the soul and reason. Since women were understood as sensual rather than rational beings, this reflection maintained the preference for intellectualism and masculinity.

In the *Summa Theologica*, Aquinas identifies women as naturally subordinate to men. He says, "good order would have been lacking in the human family if some were not governed by others wiser than themselves. So by such a subjection woman is naturally subject to man, because in man the discretion of reason predominates."[20] Aquinas notes that the female body is intended for procreation.[21] Women are, by nature, "deficient and misbegotten," and he understands them as child-bearing bodies rather than human beings made in the fullness of God's image.

15. Radford Ruether, "Augustine," 56; Augustine, *City of God* 14.16.

16. Radford Ruether, "Augustine," 56.

17. Augustine, *Confessions*, 44.

18. Radford Ruether, "Augustine," 56–57; Power, *Veiled Desire*, 133–34.

19. Eberl, "Aquinas on the Nature of Human Beings," 336, 333.

20. Thomas Aquinas, *Summa Theologica* (ed. Hutchins), q.92, a.1, obj. 2; James, "Thomas Aquinas on Women."

21. Thomas Aquinas, *Summa Theologica* (ed. Hutchins), q.92, a.4.

These theologians helped Christianize the dehumanization and subjugation of women.[22] Intellect, reason, and masculinity rose to the forefront of the popular understanding, and God's image corresponded accordingly. The universal bodily ideal reflected the dominant male social class. It became commonplace to associate the female body with sin, desire, and corruption.

Despite this, periphery movements celebrating the goodness of creation have endured throughout the history of Christianity. Irenaeus, for example, understood the body as part of God's good creation. The body reflects God's care and love for humanity, and this is made evident by the incarnation of Jesus. John Scotus Eriugena saw the world itself as a theophany.[23] Although heavily influenced by Neoplatonic thought, Eriugena nevertheless highlighted the immanence and transcendence of God visible within all of creation.

Likewise, many monastic communities in the Middle Ages believed that the purely reason-based approach to spirituality seemed dry and suffocating.[24] A rich sense of feminine spirituality emerged with mysticism and bodily symbolism.[25] Mary of Oignies, Catherine of Sienna, and Hildegard of Bingen are all good examples of this embodiment. Each of them experienced visions from God, which they bore through their bodies. Mary of Oignies engaged in extreme ascetic practices as she drew near the suffering of Christ, and Catherine of Sienna experienced stigmata. Hildegard suffered from migraines that accompanied her visions of the divine. She understood the body as an ideal form of expression for the soul, and her writings and artwork depict a panentheistic understanding of the world that emphasized *viriditas*, or the divine healing power of creation.[26]

Discovering God's revelation through the body has endured geographically and historically, even in the most challenging of circumstances. Slavery in the United States engendered profound objectification and dehumanization of the Black female body. Copeland writes, "Slavery rendered black women's bodies objects of property, of production, of reproduction,

22. Barr, *Making of Biblical Womanhood*; Byrd, *Recovering Biblical Manhood and Womanhood.*

23. Eriugena, *De Divisione Naturae*; MacQuarrie, "Celtic Spirituality."

24. McDonnell, *Beguines and Beghards*, 31–35; for more information on the discussion of reason, masculinity, and spirituality, see the following resources: Muessig, "Communities of Discourse"; Allen, *Concept of Woman*, 176–77.

25. Wei, *Intellectual Culture in Medieval Paris*, 72.

26. Jones, "Theological Interpretation of 'Viriditas.'"

of sexual violence."[27] Reduced to a *thing* rather than a human being, Black people were bought, sold, and leased at the slaveowners' discretion. M. Shawn Copeland notes that "slavery thrived on the body of the black woman."[28] Used as "breeders," Black women were sexually abused repeatedly, suffered miscarriages, saw their children die young, and watched helplessly as their babies were sold as slaves.

M. Shawn Copeland notes that bodies are marked with social location via race, gender, culture, and sexuality.[29] These social markings reveal societal power dynamics that can oppress and constrain bodies.[30] Although the body endured dehumanization and oppression, people also fought for freedom. Copeland notes that the "incarnate spirit refuses to be bound. Escaping to freedom, purchasing one's own freedom or that of a loved one, fighting for freedom, offering up one's own body for the life and freedom of another and dying for freedom were acts of redemption that aimed to restore black bodily and psychic integrity."[31]

This was apparent in the civil rights movement of the 1960s, which drew attention to racial injustice and oppression. Marxist critiques on society led to liberative movements by individuals like Rev. Dr. Martin Luther King Jr. and Malcolm X. The Black body, marked by its social location, demanded freedom and dignity. Contemporary Black theologians have noted the relevance of this in the present age. James Cone, in *The Cross and the Lynching Tree*, identifies Black lynchings with the crucifixion of Jesus. He powerfully notes, "Until we can see the cross and the lynching tree together, until we can identify Christ with a 're-crucified' black body hanging from a lynching tree, there can be no genuine understanding of Christian identity in America."[32]

These reflections shape the theological discourse surrounding the experience of incest. Historically the belief that women are limited in their spiritual ability to connect with God has permeated the church. This harmful teaching that women do not have the authority to speak God's truth in the world is damaging and damning for those who have experienced incest.

27. Copeland, *Enfleshing Freedom*, 29.

28. Copeland, *Enfleshing Freedom*, 33.

29. For an introductory overview of the development of embodied theology, see Isherwood and Stuart, *Introducing Body Theology*, 56.

30. Cahill, *Sex, Gender, and Christian Ethics*, 75.

31. Copeland, *Enfleshing Freedom*, 46.

32. Cone, *Cross and the Lynching Tree*, xv.

Overwhelmed with painful God questions, no voice of spiritual authority is given to women who have experienced this harm. In her research, Susan Shooter discovered that the predominant attitude regarding how survivors relate to God was "we need to know how to minister to these people."[33] She notes that "survivor ministry seems absent from formal authorized positions."[34] In other words, those who have experienced sexual violence are seen as passive recipients of ministry rather than active leaders with spiritual insights. This oversight creates space for the one in four women who have experienced incest to suffer silently in the pews as the sexual experiences endured by their bodies are ignored.

Such thought stands in direct opposition to the teachings of Jesus, who sought to free people from oppressive and silencing social structures. In the mother Mary, a woman's body held, birthed, and nurtured an infant Messiah. The Samaritan woman at the well spread the good news of Jesus to her village. Mary Magdalene, a woman, was the first to experience the resurrected Christ. Indeed, throughout history women have made the gospel story known.

If women, through the social location of their subjugated bodies, can make Christ known in the world, how much more can those who have experienced incest? In response to a metaphor that religious leaders are "the blind leading the blind," Shooter notes, "If I were trapped in a dangerous building at night and all the lights went out, the person I would want as a guide would be a blind person who had knowledge of all the corridors and exit routes—someone who knows their way around in the dark because they are familiar with that perilous journey." Those who have experienced incest know their way around the dark better than religious leaders who avoid the uncomfortable problem of sexual violence. It is through their bodily wisdom that new avenues for healing and restoration through Christ are discovered. Hildegard believed that the body is an ideal form of expression for the soul and thus the healing power of God can be made known through it. The social location of the sexually abused body should not merely be one of shame and oppression. It is also one of divine revelation and wholeness.

The social location of the sexually abused body prompts further reflection on embodied ethics. The 1960s, in addition to the civil rights movement, brought with it a more nuanced discussion of sexuality and

33. Shooter, *How Survivors of Abuse Relate*, 170.

34. Shooter, *How Survivors of Abuse Relate*, 170.

womanhood.[35] The second wave of the feminist movement, influenced by Simone de Beauvoir's *The Second Sex*, took on a social constructionist view and advocated for equal opportunity and representation in society.[36] A deeper understanding of the female experience, inclusive of more than motherhood, emerged as theorists reflected on what it meant to be a woman in society.[37]

Paula Cooey notes that women are viewed as distinctly "other" (essentialism) and the concept of "woman" is constructed by society and upholds patriarchal values (cultural determinism).[38] The female body, layered with societal expectations and understandings, also holds a myriad of lived and imagined experiences. In short, she argues that the body is sacred. It both points to religious truth and is itself a site of religious truth.[39] Cooey concludes that "the body serves as a compelling moral and religious authority to claims for justice."[40]

When Pope John Paul II delivered a series of lectures outlining a *Theology of the Body*, he advanced the conversations surrounding justice and the body. In his reflections, he discussed the sanctity of the human body, personhood, marriage, and sexuality. While these lectures emphasized sexuality and family and drew attention to the goodness of the body, they also served to illuminate the many areas in which bodies are still oppressed.[41]

Luke Timothy Johnson, for example, critiques Pope John Paul II's *Theology of the Body* claiming that the view is limited to human sexuality, is out of touch, and engages in poor exegetical work. For Johnson, it is the spirit, not sexuality, that is of the utmost importance when considering the body. One's spirit can intimately influence others. Although he notes that there is a difference between the divine spirit and the human spirit within the body, he argues that this distinction is difficult to identify. He goes on

35. The First Wave of feminism has been identified with Mary Wollstonecraft in 1700s Europe. Her work *Vindication of the Rights of Women* (1792) advocated for women's education. This call for education would eventually lead to the suffrage movement, which granted women the right to vote.

36. Klassen, *Religion and Popular Culture*, 96; de Beauvoir, *Second Sex*.

37. Liberal feminism advocated for equality; cultural feminists believed that women and men are different and art, theology, and understanding of the experience within society should reflect these differences.

38. Cooey, *Religious Imagination and the Body*, 19–20.

39. Cooey, *Religious Imagination and the Body*, 19–20.

40. Cooey, *Religious Imagination and the Body*, 112.

41. John Paul II, *Man and Woman He Created Them*.

to discuss six key expressions of the body (play, pain, passion, beauty, work, and aging) and discusses them from both a biblical and experiential perspective. Expanding upon these insights, Cahill advocated for a reasoned sexual ethic in society that discourages exploitation at all levels.[42] She notes that the body is tied to both human action and social location. Therefore, ethics are intimately connected to the body.[43]

Queer theologies expounded upon this embodied ethic. Jechura notes that bodies, made in God's image, are hallowed and imbued with dignity.[44] Drawing upon Judith Butler's work, he notes that human beings are in a continual process of becoming.[45] Just as God contains a certain level of divine mystery, so too do human beings.[46] Sexual pleasure is part of the human experience and, because it is experienced through the body, it is a hallowed experience to be celebrated. Jechura states, "An embodied theological ethic of human sexuality requires that desire lead to a mutual empowerment,"[47] and he "proposes a new vision for the human, sexual flourishing of all persons."[48] Nelson similarly supports empowerment via sexual identity by stating that "if we do not know the Gospel of God in our bodies, we may never know it."[49] He goes on to note that the human experience of sexuality influences our reading, interpretation, and engagement with the gospel. It is through the body that humanity seeks out the mystery of creation and celebrates relationship.[50]

These recent reflections on embodied theology have profound implications for those who have experienced incest. As Cooey notes that women have been "othered" in society and their identity is created by social expectations, the same is true for those who have been sexually abused. There is an inherent sense of "otherness" that can permeate the air when silence is broken, as if the experience itself sets one apart from the rest of society. Society and the church place parameters around the experience, either

42. Cahill, *Sex, Gender, and Christian Ethics*; Moore, review of *Sex, Gender and Christian Ethics*, 115.

43. Cahill, *Sex, Gender, and Christian Ethics*, 73.

44. Jechura, "Enfleshing the Erotic," 237.

45. Butler, *Gender Trouble*, 208.

46. Jechura, "Enfleshing the Erotic," 241; Heyward, *Touching Our Strength*, 124.

47. Jechura, "Enfleshing the Erotic," 246.

48. Jechura, "Enfleshing the Erotic," 251.

49. Nelson, *Body Theology*, 23.

50. Nelson, *Body Theology*, 22.

affirming or denying the survivor's voice and dictating socially acceptable ways to move forward.

During this "othering," the social location of a child's sexually abused body becomes multifaceted. On the surface, the sexual abuse of children is something that society largely agrees is wrong. Upon closer examination, however, it is evident that this ethic is not deeply employed as elements of rape culture persist. The sexually abused body of a child grows into the sexually abused body of an adult that is physically and mentally at risk. Approximately half of child sexual abuse victims report sexual revictimization later in life.[51] Those with ACE scores greater than four are 460 percent more likely to be depressed and experience a 1220 percent increase in suicide attempts. If one's ACE score is six, then there is a 4600 percent increase in the likelihood of intravenous drug use.[52] As painful relational patterns play out during lifelong depression and addiction, these bodies are marked with shame, blame, and disregard. Empathy in society seems to end when the effects of sexual abuse are made visible. As the abused child grows into a troubled adult, the social commentary changes from tenderness to dehumanization and disregard.

Systemically this disregard can be found in several places.[53] One such example is in the US legal system, which fails to provide adequate protection and services for those who have endured incest.[54] The failure to provide adequate legal protection or healing services for victims leads to an overcrowded prison system. In-depth studies have shown that "nearly all girls and women in prison samples have experienced physical and sexual abuse throughout their lives."[55] Gilfus notes that "a study of 150 women at a maximum security prison for women in New York State found that 94 percent of the women reported severe physical or sexual abuse during their lives. 82 percent of the women had been abused as children and 75 percent had experienced adult intimate partner abuse. Not only was the prevalence of abuse extremely high, but the abuse was also severe and cumulative over

51. Papalia et al., "Child Sexual Abuse and Risk of Revictimization," 74–86.

52. Felitti, "Adverse Childhood Experiences and Adult Health," 44–47.

53. This "othering" in society can also be found in the media, church, and Hollywood. For example, media representation often casts doubt on survivor stories, churches have attempted to protect perpetrators and silence victims, and Hollywood elites have used positions of power to abuse.

54. Haberman, "Seduction of Power," 308.

55. Gilfus, "Women's Experiences of Abuse."

the life course of the women."[56] In short, the US prison system is full of traumatized women.

It is clear, then, that sexual violence leads to systemic "othering" that seeks to "fragment" the human being.[57] This is sin at the deepest level. Rebecca Voelkel defines sin as:

> Any individual, communal, or systemic state of action that interrupts, breaks, or destroys God's presence in and relationship with and among creation by un-naming, taking away being, or removing the significance of any creature, person, community, or group of people.[58]

The embodied sexual experience (which should be holy, empowering, and imbued with dignity) results in an "un-naming, taking away being, [and] removing the significance" of the child.[59] The body, both a site and sign of religious truth, is attacked and violated. It is the ultimate act of sin against another human being. Unlike other indiscretions, which are external, sexual violence is embodied, attacking the very core of who one is. Sexual violence forces one to reimagine the capacity to know God in the body.

## HOW THE BODY SHAPES HUMAN KNOWING

James Nelson was the first to use the term "body theology," which he defined as "our attempts to reflect on body experience as revelatory of God."[60] While scripture is important, many believe that it alone is not sufficient for doing theology.[61] It is through the body that God is known. What, then,

56. Gilfus, "Women's Experiences of Abuse," 2.

57. Copeland, *Enfleshing Freedom*, 57; Martini, *On the Body*, 3.

58. Voelkel, *Carnal Knowledge of God*, 44. Voelkel explores justice and embodiment from a queer perspective. She organizes her work into four classic spiritual movements: the Positive Way, the Negative Way, the Creative Way, and the Transformative Way. In each of these approaches, respectively, she explores incarnational wisdom and hallowed bodies, sin and suffering, passion and joy, and eschatology and activism. She notes that this sin or dehumanization can lead to colonization of the mind, which can be countered by knowing oneself as "already resurrected." This creative wisdom may express itself in laughter, worship, sports, or other areas of self-expression. This creativity leads to transformation, making the kingdom of God made known in the here and now by calling upon individuals and communities to engage in social activism.

59. Voelkel, *Carnal Knowledge of God*, 44.

60. Nelson, *Body Theology*, 50.

61. Johnson, *Revelatory Body*.

can be gleaned from embodied knowing? What wisdom does the sexually violated body hold?

If experience is the starting point for theology, then the body can be understood as a source of divine revelation. Marcia Mount Shoop begins with this premise as she reflects on the embodied experiences of rape, pregnancy, and motherhood to illuminate the suffering, creativity, and ambiguity of the divine as it is realized through the body. Incorporating the work of Schleiermacher and Alfred North Whitehead, her work emphasizes analysis of feeling.[62] Feeling, she states, is "both the mode of our experience and the mechanism of our redemption."[63] It is through feeling the tragic body, the ambiguous body, and the creative body that we reconnect with the divine. In this poetic and ongoing process of becoming, we learn to re-inhabit the sacred body that is revelatory of God. Her work culminates in a reflection on the body of Jesus and the significance it holds for embodied revelation.[64]

For women, experiencing the body as revelatory of God provides keen insight into who God is. Christy Angelle Bauman has reflected on the function and experience of the female body to reimagine God-image. She explores menstruation, birth, motherhood, sex, intimacy, aging, and dying while celebrating the sacred bodily experiences of women as made in God's-image. Re-imaging God in feminist language helps reclaim the full dignity, experience, and personhood of women.[65] It also serves to redefine who God is. The notion that God is revealed in a menstruating, aging, and even lactating body changes the predominant script of a God associated with masculine ideals.[66]

Over time human beings learn about God and their world. This knowing becomes enfleshed and is carried within the body in ways that we are often not consciously aware of. Western society encourages a disembodied approach to living, leading to a devaluation of bodily wisdom.[67] It has been

62. Mount Shoop, *Let the Bones Dance*, 12–15.

63. Mount Shoop, *Let the Bones Dance*, 14.

64. Mount Shoop, *Let the Bones Dance*, 161–75.

65. Moder, "Women, Personhood, and God," 86.

66. A substantial amount of feminist literature reframes God as feminine. This meta-cognitive analysis raises questions about the practical implications God language has on the human experience. See the following works for further reading: Moder, "Women, Personhood, and God," 85–103; Sölle, "Fatherhood, Power, and Barbarism," 327–36; McFague, *Body of God*; Johnson, "Naming God She."

67. Mount Shoop, *Let the Bones Dance*, 14.

discovered, however, that memory and wisdom live within the flesh itself. Bonnie Miller-McLemore draws upon the biological sciences to reflect on this.[68] She asks, how does the body's movement in religious practice shape one's theological knowing over time? For example, "what does it mean to process forward and hold out your hands to receive the Eucharist from a priest . . . versus sitting and passing a communion plate, taking bread, and then service your neighbor? Does it shape how and what one knows or even how one conceives of the divine, especially when one practices certain body motions over a lifetime?"[69]

Neuroscientific research affirms this line of questioning. Shaun Gallagher's work *How the Body Shapes the Mind* offers an empirical and phenomenological approach to embodiment. In short, he asks two questions: How aware are people of their bodies? To what degree is consciousness, memory, thought, etc. shaped by the fact that they are embodied?[70] Gibbs produces a similar work, *Embodiment and Cognitive Science*, which integrates narratives to assess how embodiment shapes human knowledge.[71]

Perhaps the most relevant for this study, however, is Bessel van der Kolk's seminal work, *The Body Keeps the Score.* He provides a detailed discussion on how traumatic experience inhabits the body. The body will remember when the mind cannot, and it is through the body that healing is most effective. Similarly, Peter Levine's work in somatic therapy highlights trapped energy within the body that can lead to trauma. It is by allowing the body to express this trapped energy that healing occurs.

Many theologians aim to theologize from this place of trauma. Jane Grovijahn, for example, utilizes a host of Latinx and Asian feminist scholars to provide an example of how to "do theology from the body when the body is not intact."[72] She notes that survival is a theological act, and the sexually abused body, operating as both a site and sign of religious truth, can be realized as made in God's image. Grovijahn draws heavily upon the work of Elaine Scarry, who writes about the tortured body. Scarry brings the ineffability of pain into dialogue with literature, artwork, and philosophy to illuminate how experience creates stories. Scarry states, "Physical pain has

68. Miller-McLemore, "Embodied Knowing, Embodied Theology," 744.

69. Miller-McLemore, "Embodied Knowing, Embodied Theology," 750.

70. Gallagher, *How the Body Shapes the Mind*, 2. Also see, for example, Meiring, "Theology in the Flesh"; Soliman et al., "It's Not 'All in Your Head,'" 852–64.

71. Gibbs, *Embodiment and Cognitive Science.*

72. Grovijahn, "Feminist Theology of Survival."

no voice, but when it at last finds a voice, it begins to tell a story . . . about the inseparability of [physical pain, political and perceptual complications, the nature of human creation] and their embeddedness in one another."[73] Just as stories have a structure that is born from bodily experience, so too does belief.

When experiencing physical pain and suffering there is a strong tendency to reject the experience and, along with it, the body. How can hope and joy exist alongside torment and pain? Kelly Kapic's work encourages unapologetic embodiment that includes "learning to live in the presence of death" and befriending the experience of lament.[74] The embodied experience of Jesus creates space for meditation and belonging amid suffering, physical disability, and pain. Her work is a call to faith rather than understanding and offers insight into how to sit with the uncertainty and fear that often accompany physical pain. Critical reflection on human limits raises awareness that all beings are limited in some way. Rather than understanding the limits imposed by disabilities as "exceptional," they should instead be viewed as an ordinary part of the human experience. From a statistical standpoint, the experience of incest is disturbingly average.[75]

While it is comforting to say that the body is revelatory of God, it is a more challenging notion to state that God is made known through the sexually abused body. It is in the embodied experience of childhood sexual violation that God is present. How can this be reconciled with the deicide that occurs when violence permeates one's reality day after day?

While incest may be a point of deicide it is also the starting point for divine revelation. It is by entering into the experience that one rediscovers the presence of God. It is not enough to merely state "God was with you in the abuse." The questions "how" and "where" remain. Over time, in a decidedly paradoxical way, the wounds become the mechanism for salvation. It is by feeling the tragic body that one begins to process harm and unlearn messages of shame and dehumanization. By entering the tragic body, one feels the evil endured. Dread, anger, grief, and pain are all enfleshed. As flashbacks and nightmares permeate one's reality, the inner child is screaming for love and attention. In the tragic body, the suffering inner child receives a voice. This profound bodily wisdom seeks to carry out generational

73. Scarry, *Body in Pain*, 3.

74. Kapic, *Embodied Hope*, 57–62.

75. Creamer, *Disability and Christian Theology*.

healing at a micro and macro level. It is this body that knows God and seeks God even when the conscious mind has turned away.

Despite this harm, the body endures. Survival is a theological act.[76] In the midst of ongoing harm, the still, quiet voice of God nudges one toward the truth that what has happened is wrong. Alongside this survival are the very real questions that accompany a life lived after trauma. Remaining in a liminal space where one no longer endures repeated abuses but is not yet healed is profoundly difficult and important. In this space, God is known in the ambiguous body. Much like a child learning to walk and explore their world, the ambiguous body tentatively explores itself in relation to God. One must learn how to reinhabit the body. Frustration, foreboding joy, and the desire and fear of finding answers accompany this experience. In feeling the ambiguous body, difficult questions are asked of God and answers are not always freely given. Embodying mystery becomes part of this experience.

Made in God's image, humanity enjoys a higher place within creation and is tasked with caring for and co-creating the world. The stories molded from life experiences help create this reality. Stories help us make meaning, understand the world, and construct a belief system. Likewise, when the pain of sexual violation finds its voice, it begins to construct a narrative about our identity. For too long, the experience of incest cultivated a narrative of silence, shame, fear, and degradation. By feeling the creative body and giving voice to the embodied experience a new story is told—a story of powerful women healers whose bodies radiate the love of God. It is a narrative that illuminates God within the body and the body's capacity to heal. The body generates creativity, wisdom, insight, and belief about oneself and God.

To claim that God is revealed through the sexually abused body is daring and maybe even profane. The suffering, death, and resurrection of Jesus, however, offer a helpful parallel. By bringing this into dialogue with the body of Jesus, the profound implications for those who have experienced incest can be realized. The human body is sacred and the sexually violated body is revelatory of God.

## THE BODY OF GOD

The hemorrhaging woman, having exhausted all other options, broke social norms as she desperately and courageously sought Jesus in the crowd.

76. Grovijahn, "Feminist Theology of Survival," 5.

The woman, whose body was riddled with suffering, shame, and isolation, is made well by her faith. Theologizing from the location of the sexually abused body is such an act of faith. It dares to defy social norms by seeking God in the most profane and violent of acts. God, making God's self known through the body, utilizes the most painful and palpable space available to bring about healing. In theologizing from such a place of need, Grovijahn notes that it creates "new ways to think about God, new ways to find God, and maybe even new ways to love God." Doing so allows those who have experienced incest to "give voice to their God-consciousness from within the realities of a sexually abused body-self."[77]

Theologizing from the sexually abused body comes from a place of power by proclaiming the fierce truth that this experience is not the totality of who one is. It harnesses the most painful experiences of one's life and transforms them. It restores voice, power, and dignity to survivors while simultaneously giving theologians a creative avenue to challenge oppression and encourage reform through reflection on embodied ethics. It also enters the space of imagination and creativity to discover God's voice during pain. The painful things that one learns about their body amid such violence are coupled with the very act of survival itself. In this survival God's voice whispers through the body, inviting loving attention into one's most painful wounds. As bodily movement is altered over time and stories are written and rewritten, so too is one's knowledge of self and God transformed. The wisdom of the violated body demonstrates what it means to be made in God's image.

For Christians, Jesus is the ideal manifestation of *imago Dei.* His divinity, humanity, relationships, and actions exemplify the ideal life. As God is made flesh, it is through the body that Jesus encounters ordinary human experiences—he feels frustration, pain, joy, and love. While Jesus touches, heals, walks, and teaches, he also suffers, weeps, bleeds, and dies. He encounters profoundly human bodily experiences in the passion narratives. For example, in Mark 14 Jesus prays at Gethsemane. He is described as "distressed and agitated," as well as "deeply grieved" (Mark 14:33–34). After his betrayal by Judas, Jesus is arrested, mocked, flogged, and stripped. He bleeds when a crown of thorns is twisted onto his head. He experiences thirst on the cross, he cries out in anguish, and he dies.

Fear, grief, betrayal, humiliation, distress, and bodily pain are all evident. When Jesus is resurrected, he bears the marks of the crucifixion.

77. Grovijahn, "Theology as Irruption into Embodiment," 32–33.

The wounds on his hands and sides prove to his disciple Thomas that the resurrected Jesus really is who he says he is. Risen again, his defeat of death does not include erasing the wounds that he experienced three days prior. Instead, the miracle is evident in the fact that he displays life and wholeness despite these death-dealing wounds. The resurrected body of Jesus becomes a remarkable symbol of hope. It is through this body that the experiences of child sexual abuse can be paralleled. Both Jesus and the sexually abused child experience a death of safety and of innocence. Both experience mystery and darkness akin to Holy Saturday. And both can be resurrected to discover a new life capable of transforming the world.

# 4

# Embodying Death

*I was nine when I learned about my body from rape.*
*I had been sleeping and when I woke his hands*
*were fumbling where they shouldn't.*
*"You will be beautiful one day."*
*God please. What's happening?*

*The first night it happened I felt a knife tear through me,*
*unaware until that moment that my body had space for someone else.*
*"You're so tight, I knew you would be."*
*God please. Make the burning stop.*

*I remember the acrid smell of his body, his sweat,*
*of his semen as it spilled into me while he*
*shoved a dirty sock between my legs.*
*"Make sure you get it all so you don't end up pregnant."*
*God. Please. Don't let me be pregnant.*

*He tucked himself quickly back into his pants*
*I made a gurgling sound, choked on my own fear*
*as a tear slid unnoticed down my cheek.*
*"Did you like that?"*
*God please. Where are you?*

*I remember his whispering voice clearly.*
*It still haunts me to this day.*
*"If you tell anyone what you just did, then*
*they will think you're disgusting."*
*God please don't let anyone find out.*

*I never managed to get myself clean or find my voice to protest.*
*I clutched my sheets night after night praying*
*Pleading.*
*Begging.*
*Dying.*

*God please make the burning stop.*
*God please don't let this happen again.*
*God please don't let him come back.*
*God please don't let me be pregnant.*
*God please don't let anyone find out.*
*God please don't leave me alone.*
*God please.*
*God please.*
*God please.*
*Until one day I realized in my tiny, invis-*
*ible, raped, and discarded body that*
*God. Was. Dead.*

THE STORIES WE TELL matter. The framing of a story shapes one's understanding of the world and one's place within it. David Tracy notes, "The stories persons tell disclose their character. The story each person *is* discloses a human possibility that otherwise might go unremarked."[1] Life demands narrative. Joan Didion is famous for saying, "We tell ourselves stories in order to live."[2] Indeed, stories help form identity and provide people with

1. Tracy, *Analogical Imagination*, 275.
2. Didion, *White Album*, 11.

the language they need to understand ineffable experiences. Stories "bridge the gaps where everything else has crumbled."[3]

Incest constructs a narrative of isolation and shame. It seeks to crush the *imago Dei* of a person and imbue one's identity with feelings of disdain. Without intentional reflection, the spiritual wounds fester and the words of abusers find ever more effective ways to mutilate the victim's sense of self. These lashes to one's identity are tangibly felt within a body that crawls with memories of abuse. The conceptualization of this wound is critical. The story we tell matters.

The journey of incest is riddled with experiences that transcend the limits of language. Through stories, these experiences can be made more fully known. While many stories encapsulate the archetypal journey from abuse to healing, it is by bringing incest into dialogue with the passion narratives that powerful dimensions of knowing are re-discovered. Tracy argued that Christ is the prime analog or comparative experience that can illuminate all others. By examining the experiences of Christ metaphorically, a new narrative of child sexual abuse can be constructed.[4]

Metaphors are not intended to be a "one-on-one match to reality." They are many times odd and ill-fitting yet "[evoke] dimensions of reality which will otherwise go unnoticed and therefore unexperienced."[5] Victims of incest experience deicide as safety, innocence, and the body are broken. As Jesus dies on the cross his safety, innocence, and body are also broken. It is in Jesus that the wound of incest is fully honored. Conceptualizing the wound vis-à-vis Jesus changes the narrative from isolation to relationship, from impurity to holiness, and from shame to vindication. The comparisons do not always fit together perfectly, but they nevertheless give a new voice to the pain.

All abuses are different, and all survivors of incest have unique stories and wounds. Using the passion narrative as a metaphor to re-conceptualize the spiritual wound of incest may not be helpful for everyone. It does, however, create space to help one creatively rethink the wound and reflect on the gospel narrative's power. A hermeneutic of rape encourages survivors, and those journeying alongside them, to pray and strive for trauma-informed

3. Coelho, "Stories and Reflection."

4. This work is not intended to be historical-critical. It is based on the belief that the Bible is a living document that actively shapes the world. It draws heavily upon the subjective experiences of victims of incest. It is in this fusion of horizons that new insights into the biblical text emerge.

5. Brueggemann, *Cadences of Home*, 1.

interpretations. By changing the narrative, we can change the culture of sexual violence.

## DEATH OF SAFETY

From birth, human beings are hardwired to trust. Support and intimacy by caregivers within the first years of life create a secure bond so the child knows they belong, they are loved, and they are safe. These relational bonds form the building blocks of resilience and long-term well-being. Trust, however, is fragile. Winston and Chicot state, "Even though babies have a deep genetic predisposition to bond to a loving parent, this can be disrupted if a baby's parents or caregivers are neglectful or inconsistent."[6]

The experience of incest brings with it deep wounds of mistrust and betrayal that extend beyond the sexual violation. This betrayal may be enacted by the perpetrator that sexually violates the child. It can also occur via the complicit caregiver, by the neglectful parent, or by authority figures who are in denial or offer no safe refuge.[7] As incest permeates dysfunctional family systems, environments of chaos, silence, and violence lay heavy upon the shoulders of children who must cope far beyond their developmental capacity. The result is often profound pain and confusion. The damage one embodies is in direct proportion to the lack of security and nurturance found in the parental bond. As Allender puts it, "The victim's struggle to trust will be proportionally related to the extent her parent(s) failed to protect and nurture her as a child."[8] This betrayal is often too much to endure.[9]

Safety is shattered as the body is violated and the child is abandoned in their moments of deepest need. How can one feel loved by someone who betrays them and annihilates their sense of safety? This betrayal violates every instinctual and rational thing that we know. Love becomes muddied with fear and mistrust. One learns that loving oneself is synonymous with harm. The child's view of self is formed, in part, by how they believe others view them.[10] In the process, children do not stop loving others. They learn to stop loving themselves.

6. Winston and Chicot, "Importance of Early-Bonding," 12–14.
7. Allender, *Wounded Heart*, 116–17.
8. Allender, *Wounded Heart*, 36–37.
9. Allender, *Wounded Heart*, 35.
10. See chapter 2.

The road to deicide is paved with peripheral deaths, the first of which is a death of safety. Children trust their caregivers to protect and support them. As noted in chapter 2, most instances of incest occur between the Mythic-Literal and Synthetic-Conventional stages of faith. In these stages, a child's understanding of God is typically characterized by a powerful sense of justice and intervention in the world. In other words, children also trust in God to protect and intervene.

Through Jesus's life and ministry, he carefully crafted safety for others via acts of love and relationship. Leading with truth, he included social outcasts, healed those deemed impure, and taught that love was the culmination of sacred law. Like the pure and innocent child, Jesus's life was an example of God's kingdom made known on earth. It is remarkable, then, that a herald of safety experienced such a profound loss of security in his last days. Those closest to Jesus—his disciples—brought this death of safety. Jesus experienced painful betrayal through Judas's complicity, Peter's denial, and the sleepiness of Peter, James, and John.

The Gospel of Mark states, "Then Judas Iscariot, one of the Twelve, went to the chief priests to betray Jesus to them. They were delighted to hear this and promised to give him money. So he watched for an opportunity to hand him over" (Mark 14:10–11). Later, during the Last Supper, Jesus notes that one of the disciples will betray him. They are saddened and say, "Surely you don't mean me?" (Mark 14:18). In Matthew, it is Judas specifically who asks this, and Jesus responds, "You have said so" (Matt 26:26). The Gospel of John expands even further, stating:

> "I am not referring to all of you; I know those I have chosen. But this is to fulfill this passage of Scripture: 'He who shared my bread has turned against me.' "I am telling you now before it happens, so that when it does happen you will believe that I am who I am. Very truly I tell you, whoever accepts anyone I send accepts me; and whoever accepts me accepts the one who sent me." After he had said this, Jesus was troubled in spirit and testified, "Very truly I tell you, one of you is going to betray me." His disciples stared at one another, at a loss to know which of them he meant. One of them, the disciple whom Jesus loved, was reclining next to him. Simon Peter motioned to this disciple and said, "Ask him which one he means." Leaning back against Jesus, he asked him, "Lord, who is it?" Jesus answered, "It is the one to whom I will give this piece of bread when I have dipped it in the dish." Then, dipping the piece of bread, he gave it to Judas, the son of Simon Iscariot. As soon as Judas took the bread, Satan entered into him. So Jesus told him,

> "What you are about to do, do quickly." But no one at the meal understood why Jesus said this to him. Since Judas had charge of the money, some thought Jesus was telling him to buy what was needed for the festival, or to give something to the poor. As soon as Judas had taken the bread, he went out. And it was night. (John 13:18–30)

Judas's betrayal marks the beginning of Jesus's death of safety. While Judas agrees to betray Jesus for silver, both Luke and John indicate that Satan entered him.[11] In the Gospel of John, Jesus is troubled that a traitor is in his midst.[12] Still, he protects Judas's identity and tells the disciples it is merely "one of you." When pressed for further information he tells only his beloved disciple. Jesus then tells Judas, "What you are about to do, do quickly," but the other disciples do not understand.

Is Jesus shielding Judas from his companions through secrecy? Is he creating space for Judas to change his mind? Or is he encouraging self-examination among all his companions at the table?[13] Hull notes that "the identification of Judas in such fashion was more of a private unmasking than a public exposé." To Jesus, this simple act represented love's last appeal to one on the verge of perdition.[14]

Jesus's dining with Judas is a profound manifestation of agape love. For example, "Judas ate too" is often touted as a reminder to love our enemies. Christians are told that Jesus did not turn his back, even on the one who betrayed him, so neither should the church. While this open acceptance and profound love of Jesus is worthy to emphasize, the experience of incest calls one to pay attention in a different way.

What must it have been like for Jesus to dine with Judas? The text states that he is troubled to know that his friend, one who has left everything and made it his primary calling in life to follow Jesus, will betray him. What did this knowledge of betrayal feel like in the body of Jesus as he dined with someone who sold him out for silver? Did Jesus feel the weight of this betrayal on his chest? Did the burden of disloyalty constrict his breath or did his stomach churn as he chewed his meal? Did his skin prickle with dread as Judas left the room and headed into the darkness? Did his hands shake as he told those remaining about his body and blood that would soon be broken?

11. See Luke 22:1–6; John 13:27.

12. See John 13:21.

13. Hull, "John," 330.

14. Hull, "John," 330.

Judas clearly sets Jesus up for harm. His collusion results in the arrest, torture, and death of his teacher. His motives have been a point of much theological discussion. Speculation has ranged from pure financial gain to social pressure to misguided attempts to create a crisis so Jesus could seize political power.[15] In the Gospel of Matthew, Judas expresses regret over his decision. He attempts to return the blood money and then hangs himself.[16] It is difficult to think about the depth of Judas's betrayal. How can one who has witnessed the love of Christ conspire to bring about his death?

For children who have experienced incest, dining with Judas is an ever-present reality. Day after day children share space with those who have professed to love them and actively harm them. In addition to the bodily harm exacted by the perpetrator, the death of safety is made even more profound by the "non-offending" caregiver that is complicit in this harm.

Allender notes that "complicity may involve direct solicitation" in which a parent actively places their child in harm's way.[17] For example, a father might have inappropriate conversations with his teenage son about sexuality, indicating that to "be a man" one should be sexually promiscuous. During "locker room talk" about female anatomy, the father might reference his daughter's developing body. At the father's behest to "be a man," the teenage son might abuse his sister or other girls. In this way, the father is complicit in the cycle of abuse. Another example is outlined in Allender's work:

> One mother told her daughter to go play baseball with her father, uncles, and cousin. Not wanting to hear her mother's incessant nagging, the fourteen-year-old girl went out to play. A short time later her mother told her to take her blouse off so that her shirt would not be soiled. Again, the mother's harangue worked, and the girl took her blouse off. It should come as no surprise that both her cousin and father abused her shortly after the game. In this case, it should be clear that her mother set her up and gave permission to the other members of the family to abuse her daughter.[18]

In this situation, how is the fourteen-year-old going to continue? Her father and cousin sexually violated her, and her mother created the space for it to happen. Her home, her body, and her family are riddled with fear.

15. Stagg, "Matthew," 230–31.
16. See Matt 27:1–5.
17. Allender, *Wounded Heart*, 116.
18. Allender, *Wounded Heart*, 116.

She is not safe. Her parents, those whose calling it is in life to love and protect her, bring about her harm. In situations like this, the child must dine, live, and build relationships with Judas, all while being betrayed daily.

How does this death of safety live in the body? Beneath the mundane interactions and ordinary life events, the survivor must grapple with the confusing and painful reality of love and betrayal. As conversations about school and homework and bills fly around the kitchen table, the child dips their bread with Judas, silently suppressing the ongoing betrayal. Does her food taste like cardboard as she anticipates the violation she could endure that night? Does her breath constrict and her heart ache as she has a timid conversation with her abuser? With the one complicit in her harm? Does rage boil and threaten to burst from her chest? Does her voice catch in her throat? Does she even realize the complex depth of betrayal at work? Do her eyes silently beg her "non-offending" parent to notice? This betrayal is but one blow in the deicide that occurs.

After the Last Supper and before his arrest, Jesus goes on to pray in the Garden of Gethsemane. In the Gospel of Mark, he takes Peter, James, and John with him, and the text states that "he began to be deeply distressed and troubled. 'My soul is overwhelmed with sorrow to the point of death,' he said to them. 'Stay here and keep watch'" (Mark 14:33). Jesus retreats a short distance away and prays. The Gospel of Luke states:

> Jesus went out as usual to the Mount of Olives, and his disciples followed him. On reaching the place, he said to them, "Pray that you will not fall into temptation." He withdrew about a stone's throw beyond them, knelt down, and prayed, "Father, if you are willing, take this cup from me; yet not my will, but yours be done." An angel from heaven appeared to him and strengthened him. And being in anguish, he prayed more earnestly, and his sweat was like drops of blood falling to the ground.
>
> When he rose from prayer and went back to the disciples, he found them asleep, exhausted from sorrow. "Why are you sleeping?" he asked them. "Get up and pray so that you will not fall into temptation." (Luke 22:39–46)

The anguish of Jesus is evident as he prays. Mark notes that he tells his disciples, "My soul is overwhelmed with sorrow to the point of death" (Mark 14:33). He falls to the ground and prays, "Abba, Father, everything is possible for you. Take this cup from me. Yet not what I will, but what you will" (Mark 14:32–42). In Luke, the text states: "An angel from heaven appeared to him and strengthened him. And being in anguish, he prayed more earnestly, and his sweat was like drops of blood falling to the ground" (Luke 22:43).

It is not difficult to picture Jesus. As he kneels and prays, his sweat falls like drops of blood, his soul is overwhelmed with sorrow, and he speaks desperately to God as he awaits his fate. Feelings of safety are nonexistent in this passage. Instead, the narrative floods our senses with foreboding. What does Jesus feel here? Does he notice the ground pressing into his knees as he asks God to take this cup from him? Does he blink burning sweat from his eyes? Does he wipe it from his upper lip as he fumbles through his prayer? Is he numb? Or is he hyper-aware of each heartbeat as it brings him closer to death, as sorrow threatens to suffocate his soul? Jesus says, "Take this cup from me. Yet not my will, but yours be done" (Luke 22:42).

How can such a statement be reconciled? Is it God's will for God's Son to die? Many interpreters view this statement by Jesus as paradoxical, encompassing both the suffering flesh and obedience to the divine will. If this is the case, however, then we must equate God with abuse and violence. A God willing to send his Son to be tortured and killed is no better than the complicit "non-offending" parent. This God willing to participate in acts of domestic violence and torture goes against the God that Jesus incarnates. What, then, is God's will that Jesus is praying for? In his ministry, Jesus teaches, both directly and indirectly, that God is love. Perhaps Jesus is really saying "please, God . . . don't let this happen. But if it does then let your will, your love, come from it."

During this anguished prayer, Jesus seeks safety and love. He returns to his disciples. In Mark, he returns on three separate occasions, while Luke condenses the story into one. On each visit he finds them sleeping. Mark states, "Returning the third time, he said to them, 'Are you still sleeping and resting? Enough! The hour has come. Look, the Son of Man is delivered into the hands of sinners. Rise! Let us go! Here comes my betrayer!'" (Mark 14:41–42).

Jesus is praying in agony a mere stone's throw away from his disciples. Despite his sorrow and anxiety, he returns to find them sleeping. He expressed his needs, asking his friends to simply keep watch and be present. They did not. While he agonized in the garden knowing his torture and death loomed near, his friends slept. He could not secure help or even a comforting presence from his disciples in this difficult moment. They make it impossible. How does this isolation express itself within the body? Are the deep breaths of his sleepy disciples deafening in the silence? Does the isolation press in from every direction as his feet carry him forward, into the darkness? Does he fling his arms in frustration as he wakes them for the third time?

This anguished prayer and subsequent failure of the disciples to simply be present is all too familiar for victims of incest. Many have endured their own Garden of Gethsemane. Distraught and overwhelmed with sorrow they have sat up late at night, dreading the future, and begging God to intervene. As the incarnation of God, Jesus has divine knowledge and understanding. What of the child who prays for this cup to pass, who believes in a powerfully mythic and literal God? How does one disentangle the confusing strands of abuse, a seeming lack of literal godly intervention, and the sleepy carelessness of those whose job it is to be present? A child's sense of selfhood is created by how they believe others, including God, see them. God, with a powerful mythic presence and sense of justice, is expected to intervene on behalf of the child. Parents are supposed to love one through the most painful moments of life. The cup, however, is often not taken. Abuse continues and those meant to keep watch over the child sleep. Safety is shattered.

As Jesus is arrested, he endures yet another form of betrayal by someone he loves. Near the Last Supper, Jesus predicted that Peter would deny him three times. Despite Peter's insistence that "even if I have to die with you, I will never disown you" (Mark 14:31), Jesus's predictions come true. As Jesus is arrested and tried before the Sanhedrin, others identify Peter as a disciple of Jesus on three separate occasions. Each time he abandons him. When he realizes what he has done and that Jesus's prediction has indeed come true, Peter weeps (Mark 14:72).

Peter never anticipated denying Jesus. Indeed, he emphatically insists that he will die alongside him if necessary. Jesus, however, is not disillusioned. He knows that Peter will be confronted with the threat of social backlash, imprisonment, and possible bodily harm if he intervenes on behalf of Jesus. As a result, he disowns and abandons his teacher when he is arrested. He leaves Jesus to suffer this alone while he maintains his own sense of safety.

Is not this the very reality that incest victims face? They are readily denied by those who have promised to support, protect, and journey with them in life. Many face sexual violence and family dysfunction alone and abandoned as their voices are silenced and their abuse covered up. For those who choose neglect or denial, facing the reality of sexual violence may seem too overwhelming. Consider, for example, a mother who witnesses her child molested by a grandfather. The mother may ignore it or, at best, command the child to stay away from him. Despite this knowledge, the mother may continue to take the child to visit the grandparents without ever intervening or following up with the child.[19] This outright denial and neglect leaves the child to face her oppression alone. The thought of facing the reality of the ongoing violence seems too much.

For Peter, the repercussions were social backlash, arrest, and possible death. For families in which incest has occurred, the elaborate myth of the family system is at risk. Intricately constructed paradigms and power structures that perpetuate silence and oppression will crumble if one stands beside the child. Naming the violence means sending a shockwave through the social system and unveiling truth. Incest is fueled by myths that underscore the importance of silence and loyalty to harmful systems. To deny the child's voice and abandon them to violence is to deny Christ. Both Jesus and the child have been denied by those whose calling in life was to serve them. Yet again, the child's sense of safety dies.

Following this arrest and denial, Jesus is handed over to Pilate, the Roman governor. He is questioned but remains silent. Pilate finds no fault with him, and yet the crowd still demands his death. They call for the release of Barabbas, a known murderer, instead of Jesus. Wanting to calm the crowd, Pilate consents. As modern legal systems operate under the burden of proof they are, like Pilate, slanted toward the abusers. When a robbery is reported the first inclination is to believe the victim. Why should they be doubted? When sexual violence is reported, however, one must fight to be believed. Safety is shattered at every level.

Betrayed by Judas, neglected by friends, denied by Peter, and found guilty despite his innocence, Jesus moves ever closer to bodily death. Why does he remain silent during questioning? Is it because nothing he can say will make a difference to the angry crowd calling for his crucifixion? Is his silence a trauma response, part of the fight, flight, freeze, and fawn mechanisms of the human body? Is he submitting to the unfolding of his demise? Is he submitting to God's will, trusting that love will be born from this pain? Is he submitting simply to end the struggle?

How does this relate to the child who has experienced incest? What defense can an innocent child offer besides the truth? Even here, both silence and truth are weaponized against Jesus as the angry masses desperately

19. Allender, *Wounded Heart*, 116–17.

cling to the system of meaning they have created. Enmeshed in their belief that Jesus's truth is a danger to society, that they are willing to kill him for it. And so it is with the child. Rather than protect, journey alongside, believe, or even create space for the child's truth, those who perpetuate incest do all that they can to uphold the status quo. Akin to Barabbas, society often chooses to protect those who violate at the expense of the innocently abused. As safety is shattered and further violation lurks at the forefront, children often live in silence. Their voices are drowned by a society that insists their truth is a lie.

## DEATH OF INNOCENCE

After Pilate agrees to the demands of the crowd, Jesus is handed over to be tortured and crucified. It is in this space that a death of innocence occurs as Jesus is stripped, beaten, and publicly sexually humiliated. Matthew states:

> Then the governor's soldiers took Jesus in to the Praetorium and gathered the whole company of soldiers around him. They *stripped him* and put a scarlet robe on him, and then twisted together a crown of thorns and set it on his head. They put a staff in his right hand. Then they knelt in front of him and mocked. "Hail, king of the Jews!" they said. They spit on him and took the staff and struck him on the head again and again. After they had mocked him, *they took off the robe and put his own clothes on him*. Then they led him away to crucify him. As they were going out, they met a man from Cyrene, named Simon, and they forced him to carry the cross. They came to a place called Golgotha (which means "the place of the skull"). There they offered Jesus wine to drink, mixed with gall; but after tasting it, he refused to drink it. When they had crucified him, *they divided up his clothes* by casting lots.[20] (Matt 27:27–35)

The claim that Jesus endured sexual abuse is often met with resistance, shock, and offense. A close reading of the text and analogous historical sources, however, proves the undeniable reality that the crucifixion of Jesus included a sexually abusive component in the form of public humiliation and threat.

David Tombs distinguishes between two forms of sexual abuse—sexual humiliation and sexual assault. Sexual humiliation includes components such as forced nudity, sexual mockery, sexual insults, and the threat

20. Emphasis added.

of physical harm. Sexual assault includes forced sexual contact, injury, or mutilation.[21] Both sexual humiliation and sexual assault are forms of sexual abuse. Sexual humiliation played an important role in the crucifixion of Jesus.

In both Matthew and Mark, Jesus is violently and publicly stripped three times. In the Gospel of Matthew (included above), emphasis is added to highlight this public stripping. First, Jesus is stripped and clothed in a scarlet robe. A crown of thorns is placed upon his head as he is mocked, spat upon, and beaten. He is then stripped a second time. The scarlet robe is torn from him and he is dressed again in his own clothing. He is then led away to be crucified. At some point, likely just before he is crucified, he is stripped again for the third time and crucified nude. Matthew states, "When they had crucified him they divided up his clothes by casting lots" (Matt 27:35).

Roman crucifixion practices were a form of state torture intended to invoke terror.[22] Tombs notes that "Romans principally used crucifixion against slaves and other subjected peoples who might challenge Roman authority."[23] Rebellions were quelled as crucifixion practices reminded people that Roman authority should not be challenged.[24] The crucified body was subjected to brutal torture, sometimes sexually, as a means of upholding the might of the empire. Rome was known for crucifying individuals in various positions, often so one's genitals were humiliatingly on display. In some cases, they were known to impale the genitals to increase suffering and degradation.[25] Even when these practices were not carried out, the social awareness and threat of them remained. This sexual humiliation and threat sought to destroy more than the body. These practices

21. Tombs, "Crucifixion and Sexual Abuse," 18.

22. Tombs, "Crucifixion and Sexual Abuse," 16.

23. Tombs, "Crucifixion and Sexual Abuse," 16; Brown, *Death of the Messiah*, 945–52; Sloyan, *Crucifixion of Jesus*; Moore, *God's Gym*.

24. Tombs cites Josephus's description of crucifixion when many attempted to flee Jerusalem during the siege by Titus in 70 CE. "Scourged and subjected before death to every torture, they were finally crucified in view of the wall. Titus indeed realized the horror of what was happening, for every day 500—sometimes even more—fell into his hands . . . . But his chief reason for not stopping the slaughter was the hope that the sight of it would perhaps induce the Jews to surrender in order to avoid the same fate. The soldiers themselves through rage and bitterness nailed up their victims in various attitudes as a grim joke, till owing to the vast numbers there was no room for the crosses, and no crosses for the bodies." Josephus, *Jewish War*, 446–52.

25. Tombs, "Crucifixion and Sexual Abuse," 19.

were dehumanizing and aimed at destroying the victim's dignity and spirit. Tombs notes that displaying the naked victim for all to see carried with it a message of sexual domination. "The cross held up the victim for display as someone who had been—at least metaphorically—emasculated."[26]

While the biblical text clearly states that Jesus is publicly stripped three times, it also states that Jesus is led into the Praetorium and the "whole company of soldiers" gathered around him. He is a grown man, publicly stripped, beaten, spat upon, mocked, and surrounded by a company of soldiers. It is not outside the realm of possibility that he also endured sexual assault. Sexual assault (that is, physical sexual violation) was another standard practice in crucifixion.[27] It was not the exception. The social awareness of this context "was often an important part of this humiliation."[28] There is not enough information from the biblical text to determine if Jesus did, indeed, experience sexual assault. At the very least, the threat of this type of violence was palpable.

The public stripping of Jesus is a violation of his body intended to invoke feelings of fear, vulnerability, and shame. It was an attempt to emasculate, humiliate, and degrade him. While common interpretations often minimize the element of public sexual humiliation, it should be noted that if this act occurred in modern society, it would quickly be labeled as sexual violence. And, contextually speaking, the sexual threat was all too real. The sexual abuse of Jesus is a truth hidden in plain sight that has gone ignored for centuries. Even artistic representations of the crucifixion commonly depict Jesus covered in a loincloth to preserve his dignity and shield human sensibilities.

The body of Jesus is God incarnate. As such, Jesus is commonly associated with elements of purity, holiness, goodness, innocence, and chastity. Jesus was also human, and in the passion, he suffered some of the worst abuses of human power. What did his body endure in these moments? As blows rained down upon him and insults were hurled in his direction, did he stay present? Did he feel every strike and every bead of blood as it carved a path down his body? Did he try to hide his nakedness from onlookers? From family and friends? Could he feel his wounds throbbing under the

26. Tombs, "Crucifixion and Sexual Abuse," 18.

27. See the following sources, as cited in Tombs, "Crucifixion and Sexual Abuse," 18–21: Josephus, *Jewish War*, 435; Trexler, *Sex and Conquest*, 20, 34; Sloyan, *Crucifixion of Jesus*, 16.

28. Tombs, "Crucifixion and Sexual Abuse," 18.

sun as he stumbled toward Golgotha? Or did he dissociate? Did he simply endure, placing one foot in front of the other as well as he could, marching toward his death?

The chaste innocence and purity associated with God incarnate are wounded at this moment. The techniques of the oppressor aimed at violating and dehumanizing the body are effective. His nakedness and supreme vulnerability are largely met by a taunting crowd that does not see him as pure, innocent, or godly. They do not see him as made in God's image. Does this dehumanization leave him feeling broken, dirty, less than, and ashamed? Victims of incest report strongly experiencing these feelings. A companion can be found here in Jesus.

For those who have endured incest, a death of innocence occurs in the violation of the body. Acts of sexual violence can be insidious and difficult to recognize because the system normalizes oppression and teaches silence. The depth of harm incurred by this violence is sinister. Up until this point, it is the surrounding environment that has been volatile. Now, the body itself is no longer a safe space. Shame seeps into one's cell tissue and hijacks one's identity. Impurity becomes the substance of being, reminding again and again that this experience has rendered the child a dirty and discarded object. A death of innocence has occurred. The child no longer feels pure. And as the body is opened to be pillaged at will, the child learns they must endure to keep moving forward. They must find a way to dissociate to endure. Survival comes at the cost of disembodiment.

The sexually abusive experiences of both Jesus and the child are often ignored, in part, because they are "too disturbing to confront."[29] To acknowledge this violence is to accept that human beings can violate the innocence and purity of God's image. This death of innocence draws the magnitude of such harm to the forefront and challenges the church to rethink its Christology. Bringing incest into an analogical dialogue with the sexual abuse of Jesus shocks the conversation into acknowledging the impact of this reality. It is not to be written off as a sad statistic or a passing story deserving of a moment of sympathy. It is an attack on innocence, on purity. It is an attack on God's image.

The death of innocence is compounded by the death of the child's safety. Unmet prayers result in ongoing abuse, and one learns to survive by becoming disembodied. Blow by blow, the way the child knows God is killed. Incest tells the lie that one is not a person before God and infuses

29. Tombs, "Crucifixion and Sexual Abuse," 19.

one's identity with shame. Jesus, however, endured this too. Reading the passion analogically calls these painful wounds into the light. Jesus stands in solidarity with the poor, the oppressed, and the suffering. Now, Jesus stands in solidarity with the sexually abused.

## DEATH OF GOD

The culmination of Jesus's torture occurs on the cross. As his clothes are divided, he is nailed to a cross at Golgotha. Each Gospel provides a slightly different account of his death and a deeper understanding of Christ. Matthew and Mark both emphasize the physical suffering of Jesus's body. As he hangs on the cross, he experiences profound agony. A sign reading "King of the Jews" hangs above his head as the crowd of onlookers mock him, "You who are going to destroy the temple and build it in three days, come down from the cross and save yourself!" (Mark 15:30). Here, Jesus's body is broken and his demise is underscored by the Jewish belief that "anyone hung on a tree is under a curse" (Deut 21:23).[30] His last words in both Matthew and Mark are "*Eloi, Eloi, lama sabachthani*?" which means "My God, my God, why have you forsaken me?" (Mark 15:34; Matt 27:46).

The compounded harm Jesus has endured until this point spills over into this anguished prayer. Pierced by nails, the weight of his own body rips his flesh. As the sun beats down upon him and the crowd taunts him during his hour of greatest pain, he cries out the opening words of Ps 22. The succeeding verses, which further outline the psalmist's suffering, attack from enemies, and hope and victory in God do not escape his lips—Why? In his suffering he connects to the suffering of his ancestors, to the exiled Israelites that cry out to God as their enemies threaten them with annihilation. Perhaps this one line says it all. Perhaps his voice was too weak and the pain too great for him to continue. As this lament escapes his lips on the precipice of death, he is reaching for God through his agony.

Shanell T. Smith, a Womanist and survivor of sexual abuse, notes that this cry of anguish is one of the most authentic and relatable things that Jesus says from the cross. Smith states, "This . . . to this I can relate. Twenty years later, I still feel as if God had abandoned me . . . God had forsaken me *and* Jesus. In that, we share a commonality."[31] As the child bears their cross, the cry for God echoes feelings of desperation and confusion. Where

30. Tombs, "Crucifixion and Sexual Abuse," 17.

31. Smith, "This Is My Body," 284.

is God when caregivers abandon their sacred duty of love and protection, when the child is assaulted and dehumanized, and when their identity as one made in God's image is crucified? The weight of one's cumulative wounds rips the flesh like nails. Social criticism and fear beat down upon one's truth like the blistering sun at Golgotha. Culture attempts to hurl insults and discredit one's pain. And yet, even in this anguish, there is a cry for God. Unspoken in this torment are the remaining verses of Ps 22:

> For he has not despised or scorned
> the suffering of the afflicted one;
> he has not hidden his face from him
> but has listened to his cry for help. (Ps 22:24)

The Gospel of Luke emphasizes Jesus's messianic identity over and above his bodily suffering. In keeping with the Lukan themes of forgiveness, Jesus states in Luke 23:34, "Father, forgive them, for they do not know what they are doing." Is he referring to the soldiers that have carried out his execution? To the Jewish court that demanded his punishment? Or is he referring to the crowds hurling insults as he hangs before them? Most interpreters believe that Jesus is broadly referring to anyone who has had a hand in his death.[32]

This level of forgiveness can feel lofty and unrelatable for many victims of incest. As Smith reflects on the sexual abuse of Jesus, she notes that this particular passage is problematic for her, stating, "What do you mean, Jesus, that 'they do not know what they are doing'? Yes. They. Do! How can I relate to Jesus when he asked for forgiveness for his assailants while his sexualized trauma was occurring? I still cannot comprehend forgiveness for my assailant, and it has been over 20 years!"[33] Surely those crucifying Jesus knew what they were doing. They were dehumanizing him as they stripped, beat, humiliated, and tortured him. How is it possible to treat someone with such cruelty? And how can Jesus forgive so readily as his body hangs broken before the masses?

Perhaps Jesus is highlighting how his assailants have lost sight of the *imago Dei*. As they strike him, they do not realize they land blows upon God. As they strip him, they have grown callous to the dignity that God has breathed into creation. As they layer humiliation upon the body, they attempt to silence the truth of who Jesus is. As the nails penetrate his flesh and violate his being, they have silenced God even within their own bodies.

32. Culpepper, "Luke," 455.

33. Smith, "This Is My Body," 284.

Those who oppress have ventured so far from love that they "do not know what they are doing." Incest is made possible by this refusal to acknowledge the child as made in God's image. It penetrates the depth of who one is. It kills the *imago Dei.*

In the Gospel of Luke, Jesus finds himself hanging beside two criminals. One of them insults Jesus, noting that if he really is the Messiah he could "save [him]self and us!" The other criminal, however, defends Jesus. He states, "Don't you fear God since you are under the same sentence? We are punished justly, for we are getting what our deeds deserve. But this man has done nothing wrong. Jesus, remember me when you come into your kingdom." Jesus then tells the criminal that he will be with him in paradise (Luke 23:39–43).

While this passage serves to highlight the messianic identity of Jesus, it also usurps the power of Rome. While Rome takes even their lives, the criminal recognizes the authority of Jesus and his kingdom. In the most broken state of his life, another broken human being believes in the promise of this future kingdom. It is not the crowd below, whether taunting or weeping, that recognizes the possibility of future paradise during this pain. It is the one suffering alongside him. It is believed that there is a greater power than Rome. There is more than just oppressive power and the threat of pain and torture.

What a profound teaching for survivors of incest. Although abandonment and violation have occurred, there is a community on the cross. While it is of course egregious that anyone should endure this harm, it nevertheless is a reality. At Golgotha, no one understands this more deeply than the criminal hanging beside Jesus. A community exists for survivors of incest whose bodies are broken and pierced. Despite oppressive torture by rulers within the home, other survivors believe in the truth of God's kingdom. While this may seem minuscule, it means that Jesus did not endure this alone. This is sometimes the most powerful thing in the world. Perhaps it gives Jesus the strength to utter his last words in Luke, "Father, into your hands I commit my spirit" (Luke 23:46).

The Gospel of John returns the reader to a relational and embodied Christ. In it, the family system is reordered as Jesus expresses care for his mother. The text states, "When Jesus saw his mother there, and the disciple whom he loved standing nearby, he said to her, 'Woman, here is your son,' and to the disciple, 'Here is your mother.' From that time on, this disciple took her into his home" (John 19:25–27). Jesus sees his mother standing here and ultimately tries to care for her. He brings her together with his beloved disciple so that she is protected and cared for. He extends love to her during his own suffering as the prophetic sword pierces her heart. The family is restructured in this trauma. A new way of familial belonging is known.

Because incest occurs within the family, there is much to reflect on in this passage. First, how painful it must have been for his own mother to witness the sexual abuse and torture of her son! The powerlessness of the situation is suffocating. While there are marked differences between state-sponsored execution and the hidden violence of incest, there are also parallels. While there is no justification for the willful neglect of a child, there is a maelstrom of harm perpetuated in dysfunctional family systems. Are silent caregivers transfixed in horror, in helpless states, as their children are abused and oppressed? Are they also victims of the violence, to some extent? Jesus anguishes in Matthew and Mark, forgives in Luke, and protects in John. As the Gospels progress, compassion naturally extends from his broken and violated body.

In many ways, children who have experienced incest seek to protect their families. On the one hand, a hallmark of the abuse is that the family system becomes shielded by silence and complicity. At this point in the gospel story the family has witnessed the crucifixion and stands weeping and broken at the feet of the abused. Amid this profound pain, the family is reordered and new relationships form. The family must relate differently. Here Jesus uses his dwindling life to create newness out of death.

Later in the Gospel of John, he states, "I am thirsty." While it is easy to get lost in the Christological reflections on forgiveness and relationship, this verse serves as an important reminder to return to the body. Jesus, both divine and human, thirsts in his last moments. Psalm 22, which Jesus quotes in the Gospels of Matthew and Mark, notes:

> I am poured out like water,
> and all my bones are out of joint.
> My heart has turned to wax;
> it has melted within me.
> My mouth is dried up like a potsherd,
> and my tongue sticks to the roof of my mouth;
> you lay me in the dust of death. (Ps 22:14–15)

As Jesus says, "I am thirsty," it is easy to imagine his dry lips streaked with blood. His voice likely sounded weak as his tongue stuck to the roof of his mouth. And as his body gave its last breath he said, "It is finished." It sounds like a relief.

As Jesus dies on the cross the sky is darkened, the veil is torn, and the Roman soldier declares that Jesus is the Son of God. Jesus's death is, in no uncertain terms, deicide. The people, however, do not understand. This death challenges what his followers thought they knew of him. It violates the Jewish understanding of the Messiah. Jesus did not conquer like King David, establish the nation of Israel, or overthrow Rome. The death of his body kills the expectations the people had of the Messiah. As his lifeless body hangs on the cross the traditional expectations of knowing God are destroyed. Pain is introduced as a pathway to God.

Indeed, the same is true when one endures incest. One's expectations of God are shattered as the body endures sexual violation. God did not intervene and save Jesus from the cross any more than God did when the sexually abused child cried out in the night. Jesus's cry, "My God, my God, why have you forsaken me?" points to the painful realization that death has occurred in more ways than one. As safety, innocence, and God are killed, how can the child go on? God did not conquer the abuser. God did not establish a new space for the child to thrive. God did not overthrow the culture that allowed for such abuse. The way one knows God, then, has died.

Although burial is the next step and Holy Saturday is the way forward, one must not move on too quickly from the seeming finality of this death. The deicide that has occurred is not a mere flippant idea, a psychological distortion in the way one thinks about God. It is earth-shattering and paradigm-shifting. The irrevocability of what has occurred lacerates the veil in the holiest of spaces, signaling a shift between what was and what is to come.

# 5

# Embodying Liminality

*Like a hungry, starving, ghost with a bloated belly and too-thin throat*
*I consumed and starved*
*Drugs. Alcohol. Violence. Sex.*
*Violent, drunken, high-out-of-my-mind sex.*
*I became an effigy of stinking mud,*
*my wounds bleeding so loud the screams just became background noise.*
*One night with a bruised sternum in the autumn chill*
*Another rape experience made me aware that I'd taken up shop in hell.*

*How did I get here? How do I get out? Does it ever stop?*
*Finally,* finally, *I felt rage.*
*Tamped down beneath the self-loathing,*
*The shame, blame, and guilt*
*The belief that I was no better than this*
*Anger poured from every pore of my body like a raging river.*
*Let justice roll down like water and righteous-*
*ness like a never-failing stream!*
*What justice?*

*A heavy, humid, hope took hold.*
*Festering in my chest,*
*Gurgling from my mouth,*
*My skin saturated,*

*dripping with the foul taste of rot that threat-*
*ened to destroy me from the inside out.*
*Who am I? Why am I? When am I?*
*Hope demanded answers*

*My hands bound by uncertainty and fear*
*Disoriented by the darkness*
*Suffocated under the bruise of memory*
*Unable to figure out which way is what*
*The background screams developed a harmony*
*Amidst the twists and turns and black-watered rapids.*
*You Matter. You are Loved.*
*The words felt frightening and painful to hear.*

*Aching, groaning, stiff, and wincing*
*Purpose trickled from my chest*
*Fierce, gentle, warmth crowed from my throat*
*Exercising a voice scratchy from the silence.*
*I felt light begin to emerge from my wounds,*
*Dismantling the most broken parts of me.*
*A substance more ancient than existence itself,*
*I discovered love.*

Silence. Numbness. Emptiness. Grief. Rage. Disbelief. As the lifeless body of Christ hung limp on the cross, the world continued to move. The sky darkened, the crowd of onlookers moved away, and the soldiers patrolled and continued to stand guard. For the faithful witnesses at the foot of the cross, however, time stood still and shock took hold. While Joseph of Arimathea saw to his burial, the day of death turned to a day of required rest. The Great Sabbath had arrived. Death had arrived. It was finally finished. Or was it just beginning?

Holy Saturday is a liminal space marked by uncertainty, mystery, and possibility. It is a time to embrace the complexities of death and learn to remain in a holy space of unknowing. It is common in the Christian tradition to rush past this day between death and resurrection, avoidant of the discomfort and unknowing. After all, who among us does not wish to move quickly past pain and suffering to celebrate victory and new life? Very little is said in the passion narratives about what occurs on Holy Saturday. Rich theological traditions attempt to fill in the gap by drawing from snapshot references scattered throughout the New Testament. Reflections on this day often result in more questions than answers. One thing is agreed upon, however. On Holy Saturday Jesus descended into hell. It is in this dark and mysterious space that something significant occurs.

For the incest survivor, the liminal space of Holy Saturday offers a powerful analogy. Nestled between death and resurrection, Holy Saturday draws one into the unknown. This descent offers a "state of hopefulness where there appears to be no more hope."[1] Painful theological and existential questions rise to the forefront as survivors learn to move forward in the darkness. The journey is unique to each person, and although therapeutic language encapsulates the process, the true experience exceeds the limits of language.

This liminal space eludes description by its very nature. Perhaps it is because of this that it demands exploration. This chapter examines Holy Saturday from the lens of incest. Some notable understandings are necessary for a robust conversation. This chapter will first examine Holy Saturday as two notable theologians explain it: Alyssa Lyra Pitstick and Hans Urs von Balthasar. As the empowerment and mystery provided by these two frameworks are examined throughout, they will be brought into dialogue with the stages of recovery outlined in Judith Herman's work. While each of these voices offers something helpful and unique in regard to the incest recovery journey, liminality sits at the crux. It is to this space of liminality that this chapter will continually return. Together, these concepts provide a framework for analogically engaging Holy Saturday.

## THE FOUNDATIONS

The word "liminality" comes from the Latin *limen*, which means threshold.[2] Richard Rohr describes it as a "betwixt and between" space of transformation characterized by displacement and uncertainty in which "the old world is left behind, but we're not sure of the new one yet."[3] It is a repetitive theme in scripture, presented through stories of death, wilderness, and

1. Best, "Liminality and Perhaps."
2. Franks and Meteyard, "Liminality," 215.
3. Rohr, *Everything Belongs*, 155.

exile.[4] There is a "need to die to the present sense of self, to old ways of being and doing" that occurs in this liminal space.[5] It is a journey of disidentifying with the past and learning to see in new ways. This journey almost always feels painful because it shatters the way one understands God, self, and the world. It often leaves one feeling as if they are lost and wandering in the wilderness or displaced and without a home.[6]

While liminality can be scary and difficult, it is ultimately a space of becoming. It is a sacred space and "in sacred space the old world is able to fall apart, and the new world is able to be revealed."[7] Here, God is found in the insistent voice that calls one forward into this mysterious transformation, whispering *perhaps life can be different.*[8] Here, the impossible becomes possible and hope is found when all hope is lost.

The event of Holy Saturday is the ultimate liminal space. On this day, Jesus has died but is not yet resurrected. He is betwixt and between. It is commonly believed that he descends to hell and something powerful occurs. For Roman Catholics, this something is often described as the Harrowing of Hell in which Jesus descends to hell and liberates the righteous. His descent and liberative actions point to the power and might of Christ in the immediate aftermath of the resurrection.

Alyssa Lyra Pitstick notes that Christ's descent into hell is always present, whether implicitly or explicitly, in the creeds.[9] The Creed of Aquileia mentions the descent before the fifth century, highlighting its importance to early Christian communities.[10] This presence "indicates that it is tied in a particularly intimate way to the revelation of God, and in particular to the Person of Christ and His redeeming work."[11] Traditionally, the Roman Catholic understanding of Christ's descent emphasizes "His triumph over death and the first application of the fruits of redemption."[12]

4. Franks and Meteyard, "Liminality," 218–20.

5. Franks and Meteyard, "Liminality," 218.

6. Franks and Meteyard, "Liminality," 220.

7. Rohr, *Everything Belongs*, 155.

8. Best, "Liminality and Perhaps."

9. For a detailed discussion of Holy Saturday as it appears in the creeds see Pitstick, *Light in Darkness*, "Creeds and Catechisms," loc. 169–491 of 7087.

10. Pitstick, *Light in Darkness*, loc. 174 of 7087; the descent is implicit in the Nicene Creed, which states that Jesus was "crucified, died, and was buried. On the third day he rose again."

11. Pitstick, *Light in Darkness*, loc. 91 of 7087.

12. Pitstick, *Light in Darkness*, loc. 91 of 7087.

The catechisms of the Roman Catholic Church differentiate hell into four subcategories: Gehenna (the hell of the damned), purgatory (the hell of purification), *Sheol* (the hell of the Fathers), and limbo (the hell of unbaptized children).[13] The third abode, *Sheol*, is the place where the "souls of the just" were received before Christ. This is not a place of punishment, but one of rest. It most accurately aligns with the Greek underworld *Hades*, which is characterized by a nondescript afterlife. In English, *Hades* is translated to *hell* and has been generically applied to all of the abodes.

The Roman Catholic tradition attests that it is to *Sheol*, the abode of the righteous, that Jesus descends. There he liberates the just. The *Catechism* states it clearly:

> Jesus, like all men, experienced death and in his soul joined the others in the realm of the dead. But he descended there as Savior, proclaiming the Good News to the spirits imprisoned there.
>
> Scripture calls the abode of the dead, to which the dead Christ went down, "hell"—*Sheol* in Hebrew or *Hades* in Greek . . . Jesus did not descend into hell to deliver the damned, nor to destroy the hell of damnation, but to free the just who had gone before him.[14]

In this understanding, Jesus is seemingly "already crowned with the glory of Easter."[15] According to Pitstick, the church's doctrine on the descent can be summarized in four main points:

- Christ's soul, united in God, descended to *Sheol* (the abode of the Fathers).
- Christ's power and authority were made known throughout all abodes of hell.
- Christ accomplished the purpose of his descent: to liberate the just and proclaim his power.
- Christ's descent was glorious and he did not suffer pain experienced in any of the abodes of hell.[16]

13. Pitstick, *Light in Darkness*, loc. 246 of 7087.

14. Pitstick, *Light in Darkness*, loc. 288 of 7087. See *Catechism of the Catholic Church* nos. 632–33.

15. Hikota, *And Still We Wait*, 1.

16. Pitstick, *Light in Darkness*, loc. 311–19 of 7087.

This understanding of Holy Saturday emphasizes the salvation of Christ as it ushers in the resurrection. It is a view that elevates the power and might of Christ in the face of death.

This "traditional" Roman Catholic teaching, however, is not etched into creed. Pitstick's claims have been critiqued on several fronts. Paul Griffiths argues that her work narrows the Catholic understanding with technical language (such as "limbo of the Fathers") that has not been agreed upon. He notes that "the church doesn't teach very much about that matter, which means that the scope for such discussion is wide."[17] Edward T. Oakes further critiques her for dismissing reform theologians as well as Pope John Paul II and Pope Emeritus Benedict XVI who created room for a more expansive understanding of Holy Saturday.[18] Other critiques of this "traditional" approach contend that Holy Saturday is bypassed too quickly in favor of the resurrection and, as such, does not do justice to the depth of suffering that has been endured. Indeed, this is what Adrienne von Speyr experienced in her mystical visions of Holy Saturday.

Adrienne von Speyr experienced mystical visions during Holy Week for much of her life. These visions were recorded and expounded upon by her spiritual companion, Hans Urs von Balthasar. Like many mystics prior, her visions were accompanied by bodily pain that she prepared for during Lent. Rambo notes that "Speyr would often receive intense migraine headaches, as if the crown of thorns was being pressed into her temples. Drops of blood would sometimes spot her linens, as if the wounded heart of Christ was her own."[19] As Balthasar witnessed her visions year after year he noted that "a landscape of pain of undreamt-of variety was disclosed to me, who was permitted to assist her: how many and diverse were the kinds of fear, at the Mount of Olives and at the Cross, how many kinds of shame, outrage, and humiliation, how many forms of Godforsakenness."[20] Speyr notes that her experience of Holy Saturday was more psychological than physical. She experienced profound abandonment as she witnessed the Son making "trackless tracks" through hell.[21] Hell was thus characterized preeminently by a feeling of abandonment and isolation from God. No one

17. Griffiths, "Is There a Doctrine of the Descent," 262.

18. Pitstick and Oakes, "Balthasar, Hell, and Heresy"; Hikota, *And Still We Wait*, 2.

19. Rambo, *Spirit and Trauma*, 49.

20. Balthasar, *First Glance at Adrienne von Speyr*, 64–65.

21. Rambo, *Spirit and Trauma*, 50; Balthasar, *Science, Religion, and Christianity*, 134.

can experience this feeling of abandonment more fully than Jesus, the one whose very existence is of the Father.

In his reflections, Balthasar goes to great lengths to note that his theology is intertwined with Speyr's visions. He sought to publish her works, making sure that she would be taken seriously as a theologian, and emphasized that their work should not be "psychologically nor philologically separated: two halves of a single whole."[22] They first began writing about Holy Saturday in 1943, two years after Speyr first received her visions.[23] Her visions would persist during Holy Week for the next twenty-five years, and they would spend the next several decades attempting to articulate what transpired.[24] The language used throughout their writings is ambiguous and poetic, teetering continually on the precipice between death and life, beginning and end, what is and what is not. Balthasar says, "There is a total end and there is a total beginning, but . . . what comes in between them?"[25] It is by remaining in this space that their theology of Holy Saturday is articulated and, Balthasar notes, it is a landscape for all of life.[26]

Although Speyr and Balthasar's reflections on Holy Saturday emphasize the mystical and ambiguous, a few critical ideas emerge. First, Jesus experiences hell alongside its inhabitants through the act of *kenosis* or self-emptying. In Speyr's experience, hell is described as a feeling of utter abandonment and emptiness. It is a space in which one feels utterly forsaken and apart from God. Next, it is in this space of emptiness and death that something new paradoxically emerges. Characterized by mystery and chaos, Holy Saturday is described as a journey through hell. Critical of the Roman Catholic Harrowing of Hell in which Jesus descends and liberates the just, Balthasar emphasizes the theological necessity of remaining in the space of discomfort and confusion. One must go *through* Holy Saturday, not *around* it. It is in this way that one becomes transformed. In Speyr's visions, this journey is made by crossing a bridge of thread strong enough to withstand the forces of death and hell, yet so fragile that it seems incapable of holding the weight of one's life.

Speyr and Balthasar have been critiqued for veering too far from "traditional" Catholic teaching. Pitstick, for example, argues that the emphasis

22. Balthasar, *My Work*, 105; Rambo, *Spirit and Trauma*, 52.

23. Rambo, *Spirit and Trauma*, 53.

24. Rambo, *Spirit and Trauma*, 53.

25. Balthasar, *You Crown the Year*, 93; Rambo, *Spirit and Trauma*, 45.

26. Balthasar, *Heart of the World*, 207–8; Rambo, *Spirit and Trauma*, 51.

on Jesus's experience of hell undermines the inherently salvific and powerful nature of the crucifixion. Others, like John Saward, criticize Balthasar for failing to differentiate between "the *feeling* of abandonment and its *reality*."[27] For those who have endured incest, however, this mystical understanding of Holy Saturday speaks to the realities of the experience.

The Harrowing of Hell and Balthasar's theology of Holy Saturday both attempt to define this liminal space, albeit in vastly different ways. Both contemplate the implications that Holy Saturday has for the human experience of suffering, and both search for a deeper understanding of Christ. For the incest survivor, these frameworks provide both hope and mystery, empowerment and understanding, and answers and questions. Between death and life, between trauma and recovery, the survivor journeys into a new way of being. It is in the darkness that one learns to see anew. It is in the space furthest from God that one discovers the depth of God's love.

## THE DESCENT

> With a loud cry, Jesus breathed his last. The curtain of the temple was torn in two from top to bottom. And when the centurion, who stood there in front of Jesus, saw how he died, he said, "Surely this man was the Son of God!"
>
> Some women were watching from a distance. Among them were Mary Magdalene, Mary the mother of James the younger and of Joseph, and Salome. In Galilee these women had followed him and cared for his needs. Many other women who had come up with him to Jerusalem were also there. (Mark 15:37–41)

Examining the liminal space of Holy Saturday requires a return to the moment of Christ's death. In the crucifixion narrative, Jesus encounters death in a myriad of ways. His safety, innocence, and identity are all dealt fatal blows on his journey toward the cross. Now, as the last vestiges of life leave his body, all that the people think they know about him changes. Now Jesus is dead, the veil is torn, and his followers are left mourning at the foot of the cross.

What remains in this space? How can one sit with this intolerable and earth-shattering reality? How can one reconcile what they *thought* they knew about Jesus with the reality of his death? What implications does this death have for one's understanding of the world? How can one come to

27. Saward, *Mysteries of March*, 55.

terms with the horrific abuse that this innocent person just endured? How is one supposed to believe in love and kindness after bearing witness to horrific brutality? If the call of liminality is to remain, how is one supposed to accomplish this impossible task?

In Speyr's visions, the death of Jesus is seen through the eyes of an unnamed witness at the foot of the cross. This witness attempts to articulate the complex and strange events that take place after the death of Jesus. Rambo offers a contemporary re-imagining of this narrative, attempting to stay true to the spirit of Speyr's vision. She states:

> A witness stands in the space of death, surrounded by darkness thicker than she has ever known. The stench of death lingers, but the wails, shouts, and mocking have all stopped. It is over. She watched for hours as the body of her leader hung in the space of criminals. Just moments before, Jesus hung his head—defeated. "Suddenly all of them standing around the gallows know it: he is gone. Immeasurable emptiness (not solitude) streams forth from the hanging body. Nothing but this fantastic emptiness is any longer at work here."[28] Now she is alone with the penetrating silence. She stares up at the cross; Jesus has been swallowed up by the dark sky. She can no longer feel her feet. Is she standing? What is she standing on? The sky is as dark as the earth. Nothing separates them.[29]

In this passage the witness experiences dissociation in the face of this overwhelming grief. As the penetrating silence consumes her, she questions the very space that her body is occupying: "Is she standing? What is she standing on?" The darkness bleeds together, obscuring her vision, and muddying the space between death and life. Death creates a chasm, a rupture within one's being, marked by a complex landscape that one must navigate in the dark.

Balthasar states that death leaves people "crawl[ing] around like disoriented, half-dead flies, like beings whose present is submerged in the past and to whom the future blows as down a drafty pipe."[30] This land of death is characterized by hopelessness, shadows, and mystery.[31] Between the crucifixion

28. Balthasar, *Heart of the World*, 150.

29. Rambo, *Spirit and Trauma*, 55. In the original work, the witness remains ambiguous and without gender. Rambo intentionally assigns the feminine pronoun to the witness, highlighting the women mystics "whose visions of the cross strongly inform his work."

30. Balthasar, *You Crown the Year*, 90.

31. Balthasar, *You Crown the Year*, 91.

and resurrection "came the day of death, the day when life had no being. Not merely a day when life and its meaning faded for a while, when hope had become somewhat sleepy. . . . On this day the world's meaning died and was buried without any hope of the resulting hiatus ever being bridged: there was no hope of ever closing the rift opened up by this death."[32]

Although Balthasar is speaking specifically of the death of Jesus and Holy Saturday, the words are also fitting for the survivor of incest. The deaths that occurred during abuse leave this experience in their wake. It is an experience powerfully felt in the body. In the aftermath (which may be moments or even years after the abuse), memory threatens to overwhelm the body. In the words of Balthasar, it may feel as if one is "crawling around like a half-dead fly" or as if the ground has disappeared from beneath one's feet. Alternatively, one's flesh may crawl with the memory of an abuser's touch. Breathing might feel restricted as the body remembers the weight of a familiar rapist's body pushing them down. In the aftermath, the sting of the wounds lingers.

The theological understandings of Holy Saturday pair well with social scientific frameworks for trauma recovery. Judith Herman notes that the first stage of trauma recovery is to establish a sense of safety and name the abuse.[33] This journey is rooted and grounded in empowerment as one seeks to restore a sense of agency and control within the body. As traumatic memory intrudes into the present, this is no easy task. Lashes from the crucifixion do not disappear and the bleeding wounds do not clot. Trauma, like death, hangs heavy on the body.

Learning to inhabit the body is the continually ongoing task of the recovery journey. Herman accurately states that "survivors feel unsafe in their bodies,"[34] and van der Kolk states that "you can't fully recover if you don't feel safe in your skin."[35] Coping with this lack of bodily safety often results in dissociation, denial, anger, fear, detachment, or destructive behavior. To protect themselves, survivors will often hide the history of abuse even from themselves through acts of repression and silence. Even when the conscious mind has repressed painful experiences, the body continues to respond to experiences that cannot be rationalized or articulated.[36] Frequently, the

32. Balthasar, *You Crown the Year*, 93.

33. Herman, *Trauma and Recovery*, 157.

34. Herman, *Trauma and Recovery*, 160.

35. Van der Kolk, *Body Keeps the Score*, 218.

36. Mount Shoop, *Let the Bones Dance*, 49.

memories are so traumatic that acknowledging them without proper coping skills can be overwhelming.[37]

One survivor of sexual abuse states, "I felt like a zombie. I couldn't cry, I couldn't smile, I couldn't eat . . . I thought it was my fault."[38] And yet another powerfully explains:

> I wanted "real" wounds then, the kind that bleed. The kind that doctors could stitch up . . . waiting alone, feeling as I did, I realized "real" wounds could be tended. I wanted them. I wondered who it was that was thinking like this because I felt at the same time that I was dying.[39]

She goes on to explain that her abuser had "stolen something at the center of what I had known as myself."[40]

These testimonies are but a glimpse into the pain experienced in the recovery process. One woman says:

> Naming the abuse was the hardest thing I've ever had to do. It's strange to say, but I didn't have a choice. For the first time in my life, I found myself away from the people that had hurt me. I was safe. And all of a sudden these memories that I'd worked so hard to ignore were forcing their way out of me in the form of nightmares and flashbacks. I didn't feel ready. It took me the better part of 3 years to fully name the abuse. Every time I shared something new it brought up a fresh wave of horror. I was afraid to sleep because the dreams were so bad. I contemplated suicide. I drank a lot and started using drugs. I vomited frequently from anxiety and stress. The entire time I kept saying "I can't do this. I can't do this." It wasn't until I was on the other side that I realized I had, in fact, been doing it all along.[41]

The word "overwhelming" hardly does justice to what the Holy Saturday journey can feel like. Naming the abuse and beginning to move forward in the depths of hell can be excruciating. In this liminal space, there is much to be angry about and much to grieve. The child's entire world has been constructed on abusive lies that the Holy Saturday journey begins to strip

37. Briere and Scott, *Principles of Trauma Therapy*, 138.
38. Messina-Dysert, *Rape Culture*, 35.
39. Messina-Dysert, *Rape Culture*, 31.
40. Messina-Dysert, *Rape Culture*, 31.
41. Anonymous journal entry, used with permission.

away. The process feels like suffering because so much is being shattered. A painful light begins to illuminate the darkness.

The body, beautifully complex and made in God's image, holds the wisdom needed to heal.[42] As one begins to name the abuse, coping skills are built, tested, and strengthened. Anger and fear arise as repressed memories bubble to the surface. Shooter notes that "re-membering events is extremely painful since [the] exposure of woundedness and vulnerability is excruciating, but it is necessary."[43] The wounds of trauma within the body are broken open time and time again. Here, denial is resolved and the foundations of power are established as the survivor begins to find her voice.

Simple breathing techniques, embodied practices such as yoga and mindfulness meditation, massage, and exercise can help restore a sense of calm during this process. Mount Shoop notes that "many rape survivors reach a new level of healing and well-being with sustained attention to [embodied practices]."[44] A basic rule of thumb in developing body awareness is to follow two phrases: "notice that" and "what happens next?"[45] Moreover, "Simply noticing what you feel fosters emotional regulation and it helps you to stop trying to ignore what is going on inside you."[46] These are skills for one's toolbox to be strengthened and expanded upon over time. Learning them at the outset of the recovery journey, however, makes the important steps of processing possible.[47]

Although the body of the incest survivor is marked with violation, powerlessness, dehumanization, and harm, it is also marked with wisdom and the *imago Dei*. With intention and support, the wisdom of one's body begins to illuminate the path of healing. Inevitably, several questions emerge. For Speyr's witness at the foot of the cross these questions were, "Is that death? . . . Is it the end? . . . Is it the beginning? The beginning of what?"[48] For survivors of incest the experience is similar and questions may include "why" questions. Why me? Why did this happen? Why did my (father, brother, grandfather, uncle, etc.) do this? Why did God not stop

42. Mount Shoop, *Let the Bones Dance*, 50; Northrup, *Women's Bodies, Women's Wisdom*, 628.

43. Shooter, *How Survivors of Abuse Relate*, 13.

44. Mount Shoop, *Let the Bones Dance*, 51.

45. Van der Kolk, *Body Keeps the Score*, 275.

46. Van der Kolk, *Body Keeps the Score*, 275; Mount Shoop, *Let the Bones Dance*, 38.

47. Herman, *Trauma and Recovery*, 175–77.

48. Balthasar, *Heart of the World*, 151.

this? Why did God not answer my prayers? Why did God allow this? These questions reverberate throughout the body with each heartbeat, constricting each breath, written on one's skin. One survivor notes her rage at God as she began to process her trauma. She says:

> I was just screaming at God, saying—I don't want you in my life; I don't want you anywhere near me. You're supposed to look after me. I'm told you're my father. If you were my father you wouldn't stand there and watch somebody rape me and I was really, really angry with God.[49]

There is much to assess, more to rage against, and a seemingly endless supply of grief in the process. It is not a quick journey, but a slow descent as one's vision becomes clouded by the complexity of death and the weight of the darkness sits heavy on one's chest. Answers do not come quickly, if at all. There may be many periods of silence and nothingness as one attempts to see in the darkness. Dissociation is common. In the penetrating silence, the mind may reel with confusion and chaos as one learns to remain in the body through this descent.

While the survivor is learning to inhabit a body marked by violation, it is important to return to the body of Christ. Wrapped in linen and laid in a tomb by Joseph of Arimathea, the broken body of Jesus is here safely touched. At the cusp of Holy Saturday, an experience characterized by isolation and emptiness, the body of Jesus is not abandoned. Incest tells the lie that one is alone. The Christ narrative teaches that even when one is in the descent and incapable of knowing, there is an unexpected community of witnesses ready to show compassion to the sexually abused.

## THE JOURNEY

The liminal space of Holy Saturday invites us to look intently at this experience of death. What is the value of this? What can be discovered by contemplating life's most painful wounds? For the Christian, looking closely at Christ's death can provide insight into his personhood. For the incest survivor, does contemplating one's trauma lead to re-traumatization? Or can God be discovered in one's wounds? If so, what does that say about the nature of God?

49. Shooter, *How Survivors of Abuse Relate*, 58.

In Speyr's vision, as the witness stares at Jesus, dead on the cross, something begins to emerge. It is a glimmer of light without shape or origin, best described by what it is *not.*

> It emerges out of pure emptiness. It is no one. It is anterior to everything . . . It is small and undefined as a drop. Perhaps it is water. But it does not flow. It is not water. It is thicker, more opaque, more viscous than water. It is also not blood, for blood is red, blood is alive, blood has a loud human speech. This is neither water nor blood. It is older than both, a chaotic drop.[50]

As the witness observes this mysterious light, she goes on to say, "It is a beginning without parallel, as if Life were arising from Death, as if weariness (already such weariness as no amount of sleep could ever dispel) and the uttermost decay of power were melting at creation's outer edge."[51] As the vision progresses it becomes apparent that this flicker of light was emerging from the wound of Jesus.

Once this is realized, new questions emerge such as, "Is this love trickling on in impotence, unconsciously, laboriously, towards a new creation that does not yet even exist, a creation which is still to be lifted up and given shape?"[52] While staring at and remaining with death, the witness saw light emerge from the site of suffering. Paradoxically and inexplicably "death is producing something, but it is not something new; it is weary and puzzlingly old."[53] What is observed at this moment points to an ineffable divine mystery.

For the incest survivor, remaining with the deaths that one has endured leads to a similar awareness. *Something* emerges from the site of violence. An undefined glimmer of something like light flickers from within the body, pointing to both the violation and the *imago Dei.* Oftentimes one must peer deeply into the darkness before witnessing such light. Even then, the darkness is disorienting, and this new light may cause one to wince and turn away. What emerges does not heal the wounds. Rather, it provides a new way of seeing in the darkness. It is still weary, weak, and dim in the aftermath of death. It does not illuminate the answers to painful and confusing questions. It does not burn away the remnants of violence with

50. Balthasar, *Heart of the World*, 151; Rambo, *Spirit and Trauma*, 56.

51. Balthasar, *Heart of the World*, 152; Rambo, *Spirit and Trauma*, 56.

52. Balthasar, *Heart of the World*, 152; Rambo, *Spirit and Trauma*, 57.

53. Rambo, *Spirit and Trauma*, 56.

its spark. Rather, the unanswered questions and unintegrated fragments of experience are bathed in its glow.[54]

New questions arise as this trickle of light grows into a stream. For the incest survivor, these questions may relate to one's identity or God's identity. Questions such as: Who am I? Who am I as a result of my abuse? Am I more than my experiences? Can I ever be free from this trauma? Who would I be if I had never experienced this? Who is God? Does God exist? What does it mean to be made in God's image? How do I make sense of what has happened?[55] Stated more succinctly: *What is emerging from one's deepest wounds?* One survivor, having sought the support of clergy after naming her abuse, left feeling shattered. She asks, "Was I not good enough now to embrace the religious life? . . . Was I soiled and dirty?"[56] In Speyr's vision, she attempts to track Jesus through hell only to find that she cannot. Christ descends into hell as a dead man and this "dead Christ is no longer active."[57] Such questions as these may echo, filling one's body with a sense of emptiness.

In Speyr's visions of hell, sin flows like a formless river of stinking mud. Effigies are made from this mud that represent each person's sins. This sin separates people from God, leading to the experience of abandonment. In Speyr's visions, human beings have the chance to confront their sins. As Hikota puts it, "In this stinking mud must they recognize themselves."[58] It is more than just personal sin, however, that separates one from God. When one is victimized or sinned against, a rift opens as well.[59] Survivors of incest must not only confront the sins that have been inflicted upon them but must also face their own responses.

Many survivors will blame themselves. One survivor berated herself in a group therapy session because "she believed that having entered her abuser's house 'voluntarily' she had caused the sexual assault."[60] Another group member related her own feelings of shame and guilt. Together they named that, at seven years old, she could not possibly be held responsible. Another woman said, "Left with only shame . . . I had been living in

54. Rambo, *Spirit and Trauma*, 159.

55. Taken from a journal of an anonymous incest survivor. Used with permission.

56. Messina-Dysert, *Rape Culture*, 49.

57. Hikota, *And Still We Wait*, 59.

58. Hikota, *And Still We Wait*, 60.

59. Park, *Wounded Heart of God*.

60. Shooter, *How Survivors of Abuse Relate*, 13.

zombie-like numbness . . . . At 17 years old, after having sex more times than I could count . . . Terror was the only emotion for me that accompanied the base act."[61] Many turn to drugs, alcohol, distant relationships, destructive behavior, silence, dissociation, or other methods of coping. Part of Holy Saturday requires coming face to face with one's methods of survival. The mud is not always pretty.

Such questions and realizations threaten to reshape one's identity. As the mud is examined, something else begins to form. These realizations bring one face to face with the family system that has provided the amoral framework for abuse. Questions of guilt and responsibility naturally emerge. For example, in one survivor's testimony she states, "I didn't want to shame my family . . . I didn't want my father to learn I was no longer a virgin. I wanted to protect my mother and brothers."[62] Survivors must develop a system of belief that helps them make sense of such profound suffering.[63] Feelings of rage, fantasies of revenge, and docile admissions of forgiveness are natural.

As these memories, sensations, questions, and emotions swirl in the chaotic emptiness of hell, the survivor is called to simply *be*. It is no coincidence that Holy Saturday occurs on the Sabbath. Beatrice Bruteau states that "Holy Saturday is in every way a Nothing Day."[64] It is an invitation to simply be. There is no more pressure to endure violence and no demand to emerge resurrected and healed. It is a contemplative state that demands "just being . . . here, now."[65] It is a time to rest in God and to learn to receive love. In many ways, it is also a time to simply *endure*. The Sabbath is only one day, and Holy Saturday is a fluctuating moment in one's life. Despite the isolating feeling of trauma recovery, the Great Sabbath is a reminder that one is not alone. Even as Jesus's body lay dead in the tomb, faithful members of his community mourned and made plans to anoint his body. Here, the survivor is called to step forward and contemplate the love of God, found in emptiness.

To remain in this liminal space is no easy task. As Balthasar states, it seems as if there is "no hope of ever closing the rift opened up by this

61. Messina-Dysert, *Rape Culture*, 58.

62. Messina-Dysert, *Rape Culture*, 57.

63. Herman, *Trauma and Recovery*, 178.

64. Bruteau, "Great Sabbath," 132.

65. Bruteau, "Great Sabbath," 135.

death."[66] Rather than sit in this reality, it is far easier to forge ahead with the busyness and distractions afforded by everyday life. To remain in this space requires intentionality and learning to be comfortable with discomfort. The descent is a journey of self-discovery in unfamiliar territory. As Balthasar contemplates this journey, he notes that Jesus is a way that "removes every solid road from beneath our feet."[67] Still, his descent is proof that God's love endures even where God cannot go. Despite a seeming inability to find footing, the very act of remaining reveals the path.

Speaking from a space of healing, a survivor powerfully provides this testimony:

> [Telling my story] I usually claim, "All I asked God for was my life. God gave me that and so much more." . . . If you'd told me way back then that I'd still be recovering from rape now . . . I wouldn't have believed you. If I'd known or even suspected, the hells that lurked on the other side of shock, I would have tried to overdose, instead of just asking counselors and psychiatrists how likely it was for rape victims to commit suicide, instead of pleading to be hospitalized until "all this" was over; instead of telling two different but equally startled psychiatrists, eighteen months and 700 miles apart, to "shoot me and put me out of my misery." . . . [But] I have no intention of letting the rapist mangle my life.[68]

As one tentatively steps ahead, perhaps stumbling and blinded in the darkness, the story of the body is revealed. A glimmer of light emerges from one's wounds. The glow of love is discovered in the depths of hell.

It is in this second stage of recovery that one begins to tell the story of their trauma.[69] As these questions arise and one searches for answers, the story begins to take shape. Herman notes that "this work of reconstruction actually transforms traumatic memory . . . it is ambitious work."[70] Here one makes an intentional decision to confront the horrors of their abuse, ideally utilizing and strengthening the coping skills, which remind the survivor that their body is their own.

At first, this reconstruction is likely to be flat, factual, and devoid of emotion. Snapshots of traumatic memory and isolated sensations allow

66. Rambo, *Spirit and Trauma*, 73; Balthasar, *You Crown the Year*, 93.

67. Rambo, *Spirit and Trauma*, 51n18.

68. Messina-Dysert, *Rape Culture*, 33.

69. Herman, *Trauma and Recovery*, 175.

70. Herman, *Trauma and Recovery*, 175.

one to slowly piece together a timeline and reassemble a story "oriented in time and historical context."[71] However, "a narrative that does not include the traumatic imagery and bodily sensations is barren and incomplete."[72] Trauma lives in the body, and it is through the body that it must be healed. Because the incest survivor has learned that the body is not a safe space, there is a natural aversion to acknowledging traumatic sensations. The memory of what the survivor saw, smelled, heard, and felt is important. It creates space for the "storytelling capacity of the body itself."[73] It is a language that supersedes conventional narrative and points to the wisdom of the body as *imago Dei*.

Along the way, rage, grief, confusion, and fear may arise. Survivors often report feeling a "pervading sense of damage" as they find their way through this liminal space.[74] Distortions of reality are confronted as internalized lies of shame and guilt are met with light and truth. The survivor's sense of self, family, God, and the world are challenged as one attempts to construct a narrative that makes sense. It is here that one faces the darkest recesses of Holy Saturday and reconciles the trauma with one's sense of self.

In the midst of this remembering, it is easy to be blown off course. Rambo describes this experience as an "undertow."[75] It is a pattern of "recovering and forgetting" that is so familiar to the experience of trauma.[76] As incest survivors stumble through the darkness of Holy Saturday, they are brought face-to-face with pieces of the story that remain untold. They face experiences so horrible they defy language. Words are often insufficient, and the narrative contains holes brought about by fractured and repressed memory. In many cases, one must simply learn to accept this dissociative amnesia. Doing so means inevitably feeling battered or jerked about by the undertow, which threatens to drown one in the losses accrued by the trauma. For example, a survivor may be triggered without having awareness of what has prompted the episode or recall a memory they are not sure is real. If left unprocessed, this can create a cycle of anxiety that can feel debilitating. While one's learned behavior, rooted and grounded in survival, is to become disembodied and push the experience away, healing

71. Herman, *Trauma and Recovery*, 176–77.

72. Herman, *Trauma and Recovery*, 177.

73. Mount Shoop, *Let the Bones Dance*, 37.

74. Shooter, *How Survivors of Abuse Relate*, 13.

75. Rambo, *Spirit and Trauma*, 163.

76. Rambo, *Spirit and Trauma*, 160.

is found in learning to remain in the body. It creates space to identify the patterns of the undertow and learn how to ride the waves without drowning. More importantly, it gives voice to a body that has been silenced and oppressed for far too long.

As these waves are navigated it becomes apparent that not everything can be redeemed.[77] One woman states:

> When the post trauma hit, I was part way through medical school. I ended up dropping out. I wanted to be a surgeon. It's too late for me now. I really feel that way. I'm so gone in terms of my concentration and the damage that was done was so huge. I know I can't get back what I lost.[78]

In truth, memory cannot be excised and the past cannot be changed. Mourning is critical. The loss of childhood must be grieved. Herman says:

> Survivors of chronic childhood trauma face the task of grieving not only for what was lost but also for what was never theirs to lose. The childhood that was stolen from them is irreplaceable. They must mourn the loss of the foundation of basic trust, the belief in a good parent. As they come to recognize that they were not responsible for their faith, they confront the existential despair that they could not face in childhood.[79]

The deaths endured are unique to each story. The grief can be overwhelming. Many fear the mourning process because, after all, how can one hope to recover after so much loss? Perhaps the only hope is a dignified burial as one mourns and lays to rest all that has been lost.

## THE EMERGENCE

Rambo notes, "Holy Saturday is a rupture, a break, a split . . . . On the one side, there is death in godforsakenness; on the other, there is eternal life. To get from one side to the other, we need a means of crossing. But Holy Saturday declares the impossibility of bridging the two."[80] In Speyr's visions something like a thread, functioning as a bridge, eventually emerges. Balthasar is careful in his explanations. "It is *something like* a bridge; it is

77. Rambo, *Spirit and Trauma*, 147.
78. Messina-Dysert, *Rape Culture*, 37.
79. Herman, *Trauma and Recovery*, 193.
80. Rambo, *Spirit and Trauma*, 74.

*lightly built*; it is a connective *thread*."[81] This thread is strong enough to endure the weight of death and hell, yet so thin and fragile it seems impossible to walk upon as it stretches across the abyss. Jesus travels by simultaneously walking on and alongside this thread. Formed by the Spirit, the thread is seemingly constructed of faith, prayer, and community as it guides people through the emptiness of hell.[82]

Thus far Holy Saturday has been characterized by a journey through the unknown. In this liminal space, survivors come face-to-face with the reality of abuse, abandonment, and the muddiest pieces of one's own narrative. In the face of such overwhelming complexity, it seems impossible to think of love. Indeed, many incest survivors feel too damaged to acknowledge love. It is a concept that has become so mangled by caretakers that honest, compassionate, and safe love seems like a myth. Safe passage across the chasm of hell provided by faithful community and prayer seems preposterous, especially as Christian communities struggle to respond to instances of abuse. The "Spirit," however, "maintains the bridge of love at its most fragile point."[83]

As survivors move precariously across the bridge and one's light grows stronger, new questions inevitably emerge. Issues of forgiveness, reconciliation, estrangement, and boundaries with family members are likely to surface. One survivor writes:

> I didn't think it was possible to hate someone as much as I hated my father. He wasn't even the one who raped me! But he created the environment for it to happen and made me fear for my life for so long. One day I was going through old photos and I found a picture of him as a child. My grandfather was standing beside him and I could see how defeated the 8-year-old version of my dad looked. I had heard the stories about his violent upbringing but, for some reason it never mattered until that moment. I finally understood how he ended up an addict. Our financial problems, his temper, his distance . . . all brought about by opioids and trauma . . . it made sense. I felt sad for him. Don't get me wrong . . . it didn't excuse the behavior and I didn't forgive him. But I was finally starting to see the larger pattern of harm.[84]

81. Rambo, *Spirit and Trauma*, 74, emphasis original.
82. Rambo, *Spirit and Trauma*, 76.
83. Rambo, *Spirit and Trauma*, 75.
84. Anonymous survivor journal, used with permission.

The *why* questions that surround great suffering do not have clear answers. Like Job, each person must wrestle with it and discover an answer that brings peace to their own life. At this fragile point in the bridge, survivors may also realize that God's love is intended for all, even those who have caused great harm. Do abusers have a chance to cross the chasm of hell, too? Is forgiveness even necessary in the healing process? Does the survivor want to follow a God willing to embrace their rapist? Whether one chooses to cut all ties with family members or maintain some type of connection, what are the implications for one's recovery? The journey through hell inevitably forces one to examine these challenging questions.

Balthasar describes the journey across the abyss of hell as more akin to a rope that is too short to span the distance from death to life. In this metaphor, there is an impossible meeting with God at the end of the rope. Here, God pulls one out of the chasm and as one emerges from hell, death is pulled into life. It is not forgotten or left behind. It co-exists. Balthasar says:

> All of your past is like a dream which one can no longer recall precisely, and the entire old world hangs within the new space like a picture in its frame. Only a while ago you still knelt at the empty grave, a sea of tears. All you knew was that the Lord was dead.[85]

It is easy to rush past the complexity of death. Indeed, the traumatized person and Christian alike often desire to move immediately from the crucifixion to the resurrection. Rambo notes that there is "no clear seeing in the aftermath of death."[86] But it is in this space when "death and life are brought into a unique relationship."[87] This is a journey through the wilderness from death to new life. It is a space in which time becomes distorted as past trauma intrudes into the present, and when one attempts to imagine a future laden with the body's capacity to love and endure. During Holy Saturday, one learns about the persistence of love in the depths of hell.[88]

Until the survivor begins to walk this bridge and experience it for themselves, it will likely seem impossible. Leading trauma experts have lamented that the loss of healthy imagination is one of the greatest wounds inflicted by complex trauma. Emerging from Holy Saturday brings with

85. Rambo, *Spirit and Trauma*, 79; Balthasar, *Heart of the World*, 158.

86. Rambo, *Spirit and Trauma*, 46.

87. Rambo, *Spirit and Trauma*, 46.

88. Rambo, *Spirit and Trauma*, 53.

it the ability to imagine life in a new way.[89] Learning to identify, give, and receive healthy love is part of this journey. Salvaging even one good memory from the wreckage of a broken childhood can provide a survivor with enough hope to sustain them through the grieving process. Remembering a caring person in one's life or even identifying the survivor's own capacity for compassion can be enough to help one begin to shed their stigmatized identity.[90] Being believed and supported by a community of peers can knit strong threads for new relationships. Part of embracing healthy and safe love also means changing one's understanding of self. This includes holding the sacredness of one's story, complete with its missing, broken, and blurry pieces, and daring to step forward anyway. A survivor states, "If we turn hate into love, if we've turned disunity into harmony, if we've turned aggression into peace, haven't we turned water into wine?"[91] For a survivor to shed hate, disunity, and aggression against themselves and embrace love, harmony, and peace is a profound transformation. During Holy Saturday, each step forward on this path is illumined by faith as one cautiously finds footing in the darkness.

## THE TRUTH OF THE *IMAGO DEI*

The journey through death is perilous. The liminal space is scary and fraught with uncertainty. The descent into hell results in a discovery and a dissolution of previous ways of knowing and being. Victim becomes survivor. And, truly, survivor is the appropriate word because this journey toward new life is won through a fight. In this fight, one must "learn to stay with the pain of life, without answers, without conclusions, and some days without meaning."[92] What emerges is truth. Truth is not only found in the naming of abuse and evil, but also in the discovery of identity. *What emerges from the wound?* The truth of the *imago Dei*. The incest survivor discovers the beauty and power in who she is. The journey through Holy Saturday is made possible by "a dead man and fragile trickle of love from his wound."[93] So it remains with the incest survivor.

89. Rambo, *Spirit and Trauma*, 162; van der Kolk, "Body Keeps the Score."

90. Herman, *Trauma and Recovery*, 194.

91. Shooter, *How Survivors of Abuse Relate*, 64.

92. Rohr, *Everything Belongs*, 46.

93. Rambo, *Spirit and Trauma*, 75.

The death and descent of Jesus point to his ultimate human vulnerability. Before, during, and after the experience of death, Jesus's narrative coincides with that of survivors. His descent indicates that God's love is present even when one feels abandoned and alone. God's love is paradoxically found in a place that is devoid of God's love. The possibility of the impossible stretches across the abyss of liminality. The insistent pull to peer more deeply is God's nudge toward transformation and new life.

The Great Sabbath is ultimately a day to be with God. Richard Rohr states that in the liminal space one is "finally at home in the only world that ever existed. This is true knowing. Here death is a part of life, and failure is a part of victory. Opposites collide and unite, and everything belongs."[94] For the survivor of incest, Holy Saturday offers a pathway for imagining a life free from the ongoing torment of abuse and its memory. It is a journey of discovering the *imago Dei* within oneself by shedding harmful lies and disrupting violent family systems. Through the process of establishing bodily safety, naming, remembering, and mourning, the survivor walks the thread across the chasms of hell.

94. Rohr, *Everything Belongs*, 159.

# 6

# Embodying Life

*At once this body feels strange and familiar*
*Breathing as uncertain and brave as a baby's first steps*
*My voice cracking with a newfound shout of freedom.*
*I know stillness which calms the frenzy of fearful silence*
*and a soothing embrace which unlocks shackles of harm.*

*And as I grow through life, I grow life*
*With swollen feet*
*And kiwi cravings,*
*Expanding hips*
*And fluttering kicks.*
*I know God because God has breathed life into me*
*My wounds*
*My womb*
*My being.*

*Some days I am taken aback by the lashes that still bleed*
*At times I weep with the knowledge of other crucified women*
*Nauseated, still, by a past that is all too present.*
*And yet I live with every breath*

*Daring to know the truth of the great*
*I am*
*Protective mother*
*Loving Companion*
*Rough-around-the-edges*
*Beautiful Imago Dei.*

*The angel said to the women, "Do not be afraid, for I know that you are looking for Jesus, who was crucified. He is not here; he has risen, just as he said. Come and see the place where he lay. Then go quickly and tell the disciples." . . . So the women hurried away from the tomb, afraid yet filled with joy, and ran to tell the disciples. Suddenly Jesus met them. "Greetings," he said. They came to him, clasped his feet and worshiped him. Then Jesus said to them,* ***"Do not be afraid.*** *Go and tell my brothers to go to Galilee; there they will see me."* (Matt 28:1–10)

*Why are you troubled, and why do doubts rise in your minds?* ***Look at my hands and my feet.*** *It is I myself! Touch me and see.* (Luke 24:38–39)

*On the evening of that first day of the week, when the disciples were together, with the doors locked for fear of the Jewish leaders, Jesus came and stood among them and said,* ***"Peace be with you!"*** *After he said this, he showed them his hands and side.* (John 20:19)

After Jesus's crucifixion and death, he descended into hell, and on the third day he rose again. For Mary Magdalene and the others who would encounter the risen Christ, the resurrection is terrifying, joyous, and impossible. Throughout the Gospels, the resurrected Jesus soothes the fear of his followers by inviting them to witness his wounds and embrace peace. While his followers do not recognize him at first, soon they come to understand his identity in a new way. They see and touch his wounds, they converse, they share a meal, and they go on to share the good news of his ministry and defeat over death. Their encounter with the resurrected Christ surpasses the boundaries of logic and language, demanding them to reconstruct their knowledge of who Jesus is. Now, they must *be* and *know* differently in the wake of this truth.

Encountering the resurrected Christ undoubtedly made the disciples revisit the basic question of his identity. Who *is* this Jesus, this Son of God? How does one's understanding of his teachings change with belief in his resurrection? What are the implications for all of humanity? Theologians as far back as Irenaeus and Augustine have held Jesus up as the ideal form of one made in God's image.[1] So what does it mean to say that humanity is made in God's image? Jesus, the ideal model of the *imago Dei*, lives again despite his death-dealing wounds. He appears pierced yet whole. How can one so broken and crucified by oppressive abusers know the wholeness and beauty of God? Parker Palmer notes that "wholeness does not mean perfection; it means embracing brokenness as an integral part of life."[2] Just as resurrection was born from the crucifixion, so too can survivors of incest "use devastation as a seedbed for new life."[3]

Living in the brutal aftermath of incest and trauma, it seems ludicrous to believe in resurrection. The possibility that new life can grow and flourish in a body ravaged and repeatedly defiled merits a scoff, an eye-roll, and perhaps even some rage.[4] After all, how can someone dare to claim there is life after such ongoing death if they themselves have not lived it?[5] For the disciples encountering the resurrected Christ, it took tangible experience to overcome their disbelief, and still they questioned. In spaces such as this, one is invited to wonder about the resurrected body of Christ.[6] What was it like to live in a body replete with death? Such ruminations can illuminate the survivor's journey in profoundly new ways.[7]

Consider, for example, if the resurrected Jesus ever reflected on his wounds before ascending to heaven. Did he ever pause to contemplate the holes in his hands and feet? Did he ever touch his side and flinch at the memory of his body being broken for all to see? Perhaps he looked at his naked body and remembered the sting of shame as he was stripped in the streets? Or shivered at the threat of sexual violation. Did he remember the

1. Weinandy, "St. Irenaeus and the *Imago Dei*," 19; Mattox, "Augustine."
2. Palmer, *Hidden Wholeness*, 5.
3. Palmer, *Hidden Wholeness*, 5.
4. Smith, "This Is My Body," 278–86.
5. Women of Magdalene and Stevens, *Find Your Way Home*, 80.
6. Hurtig Casbon and Hare, "Bringing the Book to Life," 218.
7. Tracy, *Analogical Imagination*, 233.

voices of those taunting him, the cries of his mother at the foot of his cross, or the stench of death as it circled him at Golgotha?

Let us hope so. Because if he did, then that means he could also reflect on how his identity changed. On how he transformed in the eyes of society from a hillbilly Galilean, carpenter's son, and crazy prophet to a change-maker, healer, and Son of God. From one whose body was broken and bleeding to one whose body provides hope beyond imagination. If he reflected then he understood what it was like to find life again in a brutalized body. He knew that for some, like Thomas, witnessing his wounds would help them believe that life has more possibilities than one could ever imagine. He knew that the holes where the nails pierced his hands would help him hold others more gently and his wounded feet would teach him to walk with purpose. With every breath taken from his gaping side, he would understand how to calm the resurgence of memory and trust in the stillness of God.

The time between Jesus's death, descent, and resurrection was relatively short. Perhaps he did not have time to linger in contemplation. Survivors of incest, however, do. As one learns to make safe a body that has oppressed and continues to oppress with memory, the resurrected body of Jesus invites wonder and contemplation. So often it is easy to feel like an imposter in the resurrected life. Sometimes feeling as if "healing" is a far-off fantasy every time an unwanted memory bubbles to the surface, disqualifying one from a life wholly lived. It is almost as if the lies of abusers scream through anxiety attacks attempting to arrest and crucify survivors with their memories all over again.

But if the Son of God found new life with his wounds, and humanity is made in God's image, then this means we can also flourish. Like the resurrected Christ, we can experience the liberating knowledge of ourselves made in God's image. It is an authoritative embodied truth, made known even in the throes of memory. The *imago Dei* within reminds us that our capacity to remember, know, and love God has not been destroyed by sexual violation. Like the resurrected Christ, it equips one with the power to transform the world. Returning to wonder, the sexually abused survivor meets the resurrected Christ in his lingering wounds.

In the opening lines of this work, it was established that child sexual abuse in the form of incest is a trauma so profound that it can be likened to death. The child is dehumanized at the hands of one's family, their body used and broken by the sins of others. Christ's body breaks and bleeds to bless others, affirming his divine identity. The child, however, embodies a desecration and inversion of the Eucharist. They emerge cursed, navigating a world filled with fear and loss. As the Eucharist teaches us that Christ has saved us, the child's broken body is taught that salvation is a myth. The paradigms constructed about God are destroyed. Deicide ensues.

Holy Saturday, however, offers the transformative power of liminality. Descending into hell submerges one in mystery and discovery as one is brought face to face with painful questions and incomprehensible realities. The hard work of naming, remembering, and mourning one's story gives shape and cohesion to a fragmented childhood. As one encounters the stinking mud of hell one begins to see the sins of others as well as the messy ways one fought to survive. Holy Saturday provides the opportunity to disentangle complex experiences and learn to rest in uncertainty. As one journeys across this chasm of hell and begins to emerge, the hope of resurrection shines brightly.

But what does it mean to be resurrected? Does it allow one to forget wounds and live as if they never occurred? Or is it more apt that one learns to live freely, emerging out of the harm done? How does one accept the promise of restoration after encountering the depths of death and hell? How can new life emerge from the stinking rivers of mud discovered on Holy Saturday? The capacity to imagine a new life in the aftermath of trauma plants a seed of hope. The greatest liberative tool of the survivor is the experiential knowledge of one's self made in the image of God.

One survivor of abuse notes the challenge and truth of the *imago Dei.* She says,

> It is hard for me to believe that I was made in the image of God. Lately, though, when I look in the mirror I can see God's child. I can look deep into her eyes and see that under the pain is courage, love, acceptance, willingness, open-mindedness, joy, self-worth, honesty, peace, truth, faith, humility, and my true self . . . . A time will come when you don't want to go on, but going on is a wonderful path that you can't even imagine. Today I say hold on to the one thing and that is self. You were made in God's image.[8]

While resurrection illuminates this truth, it is a hard-won path birthed from encounters with radical love. As the last and continuing stage of Christ's journey, resurrection illuminates the *imago Dei* and sets forth a path for survivors to remember, know, and love God within themselves. It is inherently

8. Women of Magdalene and Stevens, *Find Your Way Home*, 20.

creative and action-oriented, illuminating aspects of one's body, identity, and potential previously oppressed by trauma. Resurrection is the lotus emerging from mud allowing the survivor to see themselves as God sees them. Resurrected in a body marked by violation, Jesus's narrative illuminates the possibilities for the survivor of incest. This chapter will explore the resurrection of the wounded body and transformed identity. Weaving memory throughout one is prompted to wonder about the *imago Dei*.

## RESURRECTION OF THE WOUNDED BODY

By the end of the Sabbath, the followers of Jesus were left to sit with their grief. His death was real. His body lay wrapped in a burial shroud in the tomb. Some, like Mary Magdalene, visited the tomb early Sunday morning with spices and anointing oils, intending to honor his broken body while processing their own pain.[9] In Luke, some disciples traveled along the road to Emmaus and discussed what had transpired.[10] John tells the story of the disciples huddled in fear in an upper room, fearful of the powers that just crucified their teacher.[11] In each telling of the resurrection narrative, the followers of Christ are caught in the throes of pain.

When Jesus appears, he is not immediately recognized. Mary Magdalene mistakes him for the gardener at first. She recognizes him by his voice when he speaks her name.[12] He walks alongside some disciples on the road to Emmaus, and he is recognized when he eats with them.[13] In the upper room, the disciples see his wounds. He shows them his hands and feet. He invites them to touch his body and believe that he is real.[14] The resurrected Jesus is not merely an apparition or a vision. Although wounded, violated, abused, and buried . . . he is alive. Despite all that he has endured he meets the people amid their pain. He appears as they mourn, process, and fear what is to come. What results is a dramatic epistemological shift for the followers of Christ.

Well into the healing journey and after the depths of Holy Saturday, survivors of incest will still find themselves occasionally caught in the

9. Matt 28:1.

10. Luke 24:13–35.

11. John 20:19–23.

12. John 20:16.

13. Luke 24:41–43.

14. Luke 24:39; John 20:26–27.

undertow of trauma.[15] Grief, pain, and fear arise intermittently throughout the journey, manifesting in various ways.[16] Sometimes, just when it seems that "healing" has been achieved something intrudes to remind us that there is still hard and holy work to be done. There are many learned behaviors that one is apt to call upon such as confining oneself in fear, getting lost in rumination, isolating in grief, or engaging in self-destructive behaviors. Victims of incest, in particular, "may anesthetize their sexuality and then feel intensely ashamed if they become excited by sensations or images that recall their molestation."[17] When triggered or faced with discussing the experience, "one person's blood pressure may increase while another responds with the beginnings of a migraine headache. Still others may shut down emotionally."[18] In the midst of such setbacks it is easy to feel disqualified from the resurrected life. There is often the misguided belief that to be "healed" or resurrected means to exist without the burden of one's experiences. But Jesus appears wounded, carrying the experiential knowledge of his trauma.

The Gospel narratives teach us that it is precisely in these moments that love breaks through and demands a different way of knowing and being. In Fowler's work on faith development, he notes that significant change in one's faith often comes as a result of reconstructive or intrusive change.[19] He says, "The need or imperative for deep-going change in our lives usually comes in response to some experience of shipwreck, of failure in love or work, or of spiritual struggle or illumination . . . . Reconstructive work in our lives [is] made necessary by the legacy of wounds, warps, or fallibilities which become part of our selfhood in the processes of our growth and development."[20]

The resurrection appearance presented such a radical shift, an intrusive change in the disciples' lives that altered their way of knowing. They are faced with the reality that their current mode of operation is inefficient. They cannot move forward by hiding in fear. They cannot walk toward a new life by ruminating continually about the old one. The appearance of

15. Van der Kolk, *Body Keeps the Score*, 67.
16. Van der Kolk, *Body Keeps the Score*, 67.
17. Van der Kolk, *Body Keeps the Score*, 67.
18. Van der Kolk, *Body Keeps the Score*, 67.
19. Fowler, *Faith Development*, loc. 1152 of 1515.
20. Fowler, *Faith Development*, loc. 1191 of 1515.

the resurrected Christ forces them to reconfigure how they live and how they see. It brings about a fundamental reconstruction of reality.

The first Easter represents a defeat of the oppressors' most brutal weapon—death. It projects power and agency in the wake of torment, demonstrating that new life is possible. Jesus does not accomplish this by show of force. He does not obliterate Rome. He does not arrive in a blazing chariot to proclaim his glory. He does not blast apart the tomb. Instead, he meets people in their pain and reminds them about love. His gentle appearance, unrecognized at first, brings with it the promise that death can be defeated *and* reminds the disciples of his teachings. The disciples traveled with Jesus throughout his ministry and witnessed his love for others and themselves along the way. It is his reappearance, the reappearance of love, that marks the shift in their understanding. It is this love that changes how they see both the wounds of Christ and themselves.

This shift is not easy. Indeed, during this reconstruction, his appearance is naturally met with disbelief, doubt, and awe. Matthew says, "When they saw him, they worshipped him; but some doubted" (Matt 28:17), and in Luke the disciples are initially "startled and frightened, thinking they saw a ghost" (Luke 24:37). Although full of love, his appearance shipwrecks all that they think they know about life. In this, he invites the disciples to look at his wounds and believe. They are challenged to grow and develop in new ways. In John, Thomas says, "Unless I see the nail marks in his hands and put my finger where the nails were, and put my hand into his side, I will not believe" (John 20:25). Thomas is often ridiculed for his need for proof, but perhaps it is his response that offers the most palpable connection to the risen body of Christ. As his basic world views about life and death shift, it is to the body that he turns for answers. It is the wounds that anchor him to this new reality. It is by gazing at the broken yet living body of Christ that the veil is lifted from the disciple's eyes. It is by his penetrated skin that his divine power is made known.

The wounded body of Jesus holds a profound capacity for storytelling.[21] Each mark embodies a memory replete with sensation, emotion, and experience that informs his way of being in the world. In his resurrection, some of his wounds remain while others are either healed or not mentioned. Particular attention is drawn to his hands, feet, and side. These are the most striking wounds, having held his body captive on the cross and pierced him to assure his death. These are the wounds that make one

21. Mount Shoop, *Let the Bones Dance*, 37.

cringe with pain at the thought of their infliction and serve as some of the most profound symbols for Christianity. These wounds stand out, palpably speaking to the atrocities of crucifixion. In these marks, Jesus's body tells the story of brutality and death.

Jesus, however, appears resurrected with these marks of death. In doing so, the story told by the body changes. He lives despite these wounds. It is by these wounds that others believe, witness the possibility of new life, and come to know the world in a profoundly new way. These wounds create community. They soothe the grief of Mary at the tomb, foster belonging on the journey to Emmaus, and defeat fear in the upper room. The resurrection of the crucified body tells a story that invites us to imagine the impossible. A dead man can live. Tools of torment can come to represent hope. Oppressive systems that torture the innocent with weapons of fear and violation are not as mighty as they once seemed. The body of Jesus tells the transformative story of how new life can emerge from devastation.[22]

Survivors of incest, of course, have similar wounds. Some experiences are more palpable than others, standing out vividly in the mind and marking the body in ways reminiscent of death. Often the most distressing wound is the memory of the first penetration, when a child's innermost being is violated by the abuser. Sometimes the wound is a sensation, smell, or sound associated with a traumatic event.[23] Unlike Jesus, however, these marks are not visible on the skin for all to see. While the disciples peer into Jesus's side seeking understanding, society tends to actively avert the gaze away from the wounds of incest. Consider, for example, the story of a ten-year-old child forced to travel across state lines to seek an abortion after being raped.[24] Much moral outrage focused on the act of abortion rather than on the brutal violation of the child.[25] The innocent child is publicly crucified as the crowd cries for justice.

The wounds of child sexual abuse that bleed and fester in the wake of rape culture are often hidden in plain sight, unrecognized under the judgmental gaze. Addiction, promiscuity, dysfunction, and poor health outcomes cover the skin like a blanket of dried blood and shame.[26] As one's

22. Palmer, *Hidden Wholeness*, 5.

23. Herman, *Trauma and Recovery*, 42; Levine, *Waking the Tiger*, 147–49; Coleman, *Dinah Project*, 12–13.

24. Da Silva, "Man Indicted in Rape of Ohio Girl."

25. McCammon and Sullivan, "Indiana Doctor."

26. Felitti, "Relation Between," 44–47.

self-image and God-image are harmed, the child endures and grows up to embody this ongoing death. It is only by bathing such wounds in the light of recognition that they can be healed. Somehow, the child learns to live.[27]

The promise of resurrection invites something to break into this living death and demand a new way of knowing. This intrusive change is often brought about by the experience of safety or love.[28] In the Gospels, Jesus is this embodiment of love. For Mary Magdalene, gripped by her grief, love greets her by name. For the disciples processing their experience on the road to Emmaus, love illuminates old teachings in new ways. For the disciples hiding in fear in the upper room, love breaks in. For survivors of incest that have embodied fear and oppression, the concepts of safety and love have been corrupted, sexualized, and overlaid with shame.[29] Nevertheless, love intrudes.

Love that brings resurrection is not Pollyanna or unrealistic. It is not adorned in glitter, offering the promise of a new life free from suffering. It is not easily recognized or trusted. It is a safe space built from the grit of life and adorned with community pains. It looks like a change of clothes provided to an addict looking for her next fix or befriending a social pariah. One survivor notes how her journey to new life started with a bag of chips:

> I used to walk around the neighborhood where one of the [recovery] communities was located. I was scared to go near the house and so were the other women and drug dealers. Then one day someone . . . offered me a soda and a bag of chips and told me if I ever got tired there was a place for me. About a week later she gave me more food and kept offering me a place to come and rest. It was the greatest example of hospitality that I have ever witnessed. It finally took root, and one day I crossed the street and made my way up the steps and knocked on the door. When I left two years later with a full-time job, a car, and an apartment, I thought about how it all had started with someone offering me a bag of chips.[30]

Although survivors are often not quick to trust, persistent encounters with love provide the courage to look and feel in new ways. It is love that allows one to emerge from the chasm of hell, their wounds bearing witness to the

27. Mount Shoop, *Let the Bones Dance*, 57.

28. Fowler, *Faith Development*, loc. 1152 of 1515; Coleman, *Dinah Project*, 5.

29. Allender, *Wounded Heart*, 48–50.

30. Women of Magdalene and Stevens, *Find Your Way Home*, 61. The survivor here is referring to the Thistle Farms community of Magdalene.

experience but no longer festering in silence and pain. Love fosters resurrection and from our own wounds pull others from the depths.

While some of Jesus's wounds rise to the forefront of the resurrection discussion, others remain notably absent. The cuts on his forehead from the crown of thorns, the lashes on his back, and the miscellaneous bruises and scrapes that he surely acquired throughout the passion are conspicuously unmentioned in the biblical texts. Is their continued presence implied alongside the punctured hands and feet? Are these wounds healed? Or are they simply left out, unimportant, in the larger scheme of the story?

Although these wounds fade into the textual background, they have been vividly captured in the artistic memory of Christian history. Nineteenth-century Austrian painter Josef Kastner, for example, captures the resurrected Christ with a golden halo illuminating the crown of thorns and blood.[31] Another eighteenth-century German school oil painting shows the body of the resurrected Christ with streaks of blood dripping down his legs, arms, and head.[32] Here, images capture what words cannot. Although some wounds slip beneath the tide of fickle memory, their presence remains vividly known to the survivor. The body still recalls a touch, smell, a whisper of pain akin to the flow of dried blood on Christ's skin.

As one attempts to paint a picture of abuse with certainty one may notice that there are large swaths of life that cannot be remembered. The good often disappears with the bad.[33] This episodic amnesia may feel like a curse as one searches for meaning and understanding. Recognizing this is part of the mourning process as one grieves a childhood that has, quite literally, been lost.[34] Traumatic memory is stored differently than ordinary memory and thus hides like a shadow beneath the throes of dissociation.[35] Fearing that the memories cannot be trusted due to their dream-like qualities, portions of one's childhood become a blur.[36] While one must come to terms with how to live with this ambiguity and absence, traumatic memory remains stored in the body. The artwork of Jesus captures the lashes on his skin just as the body of the incest survivor remembers the violating touch.

31. Kastner, *Resurrected Christ.*

32. German School, *Resurrection of Jesus Christ.*

33. Van der Kolk, *Body Keeps the Score*, 192–94.

34. Herman, *Trauma and Recovery*, 176–81.

35. Van der Kolk, *Body Keeps the Score*, 192–96; Paul, "How Traumatic Memories Hide."

36. Damis, "Role of Implicit Memory," 71; Loftus, "Planting Misinformation," 361–66.

It is in the act of remembering, even when one doubts, that meaning is found. According to van der Kolk, "As long as memory is inaccessible, the mind is unable to change it. But as soon as a story starts being told, particularly if it is told repeatedly, it changes—the act of telling itself changes the tale. The mind cannot help but make meaning out of what it knows."[37]

In the throes of resurrection, a narrative is crafted from the fragments.[38] Sifting through the ambiguity of memory can lead to awe. A survivor powerfully explains this experience.

> In retrospect, I feel about my life the way some people feel about war. If you survive, then it becomes a good war. Danger makes you active, it makes you alert, it forces you to experience and thus to learn. I know now the cost of my life, the real price that has been paid. Contact with inner pain has immunized me against most petty hurts. Hopes I still have in abundance, but very few needs. My pride of intellect has been shattered. If I didn't know about half of my own life, what other knowledge can I trust? Yet even here I see a gift, for in place of my narrow, pragmatic world of cause and effect . . . I have burst into an infinite world full of wonder.[39]

To be sure, the survivor of incest certainly experienced unspeakable tragedies in the forgotten fragments. At a certain point, recalling and placing memories along a timeline of abuse seems inconsequential. But what if, in the gaps, one also met a teacher who instilled a love of poetry through their compliments, making one's heart glow with pride? What if in the murky memory lies the experience of unbridled joy escaping in full-belly laughter? Although the ages of six to ten are lost in a fog, surely in the midst one's body feels the excitement of cracking the spine of a new book or feeling the soft fur of a beloved pet. One woman reflects on her healing journey by saying:

> The change for me was to love my thoughts and even my memories. I remember the day I went to church and my grandmother sent me with her blessing, saying, "You must praise the Lord." I am loving that memory. I am praising the little pink dress and white shoes I wore that Sunday. I am praising how big the church doors were and how small I was. That memory may not seem important, but it is enough to change me.[40]

37. Van der Kolk, *Body Keeps the Score*, 193.
38. Herman, *Trauma and Recovery*, 176–81.
39. Herman, *Trauma and Recovery*, 213; Fraser, *My Father's House*, 253.
40. Women of Magdalene and Stevens, *Find Your Way Home*, 40.

Although these losses are to be grieved, there is also hope and love to be recovered. Examining the possibility of such occurrences opens one up to a world of wonder.[41] Pope Benedict XVI has powerfully noted that "memory and hope are inseparable."[42]

And while Jesus endured much suffering on the way to the cross, some wounds undoubtedly paled in comparison to others. Not all blows were fatal. Not every lash landed nor did every insult sting. The memory of a taunt collapses under the weight of the cross. The taste of blood and sweat washes away in the rush of sour wine and gall (a combination, by the way, meant to ease suffering as one nears death).[43] This forgetfulness is a hallmark of the mind's capacity to protect and heal.[44] Here, the body's capacity for storytelling sometimes omits and edits pieces of the narrative to help us be "more at home with ourselves."[45]

And so, in resurrection the survivor is invited to acknowledge the missing pieces and then "hear and marvel at the genius of our bodies in the wake of trauma."[46] Not every experience needs to be remembered and named on the healing journey.[47] Although the body holds wisdom, there is freedom in the mind's capacity to let some things go.[48] It is a freedom that can be felt in the body whose heart beats despite all that has been endured. There is awe in the possibility of forgotten joy and hope. A warm glow or the eruption of unexpected laughter points one to the life God intended. There is beauty in the promise that not all wounds will linger. Some will even be forgotten.

As one persistently encounters safety and love, the wounds of shame that hang invisibly upon the body begin to fade. The power taken away as Jesus was stripped and violated is restored through acts of agency. In the Gospel of John Jesus appears to Mary Magdalene and says to her, "Do not hold

41. Herman, *Trauma and Recovery*, 202–4.

42. Eden, *My Peace I Give You*, 4; Ratzinger, *Seek That Which Is Above*, 15.

43. Youssef, "Sour Wine and Gall."

44. Van der Kolk, *Body Keeps the Score*, 182.

45. Mount Shoop, *Let the Bones Dance*, 37.

46. Mount Shoop, *Let the Bones Dance*, 37.

47. Van der Kolk, *Body Keeps the Score*, 255. See, particularly, van der Kolk's entire chapter on EMDR. There is evidence that one can heal from acute and chronic trauma without verbalizing it by utilizing EMDR. Complex trauma such as incest, however, benefits most from a mixed-methods approach that utilizes EMDR as well as somatic and talk therapy. In EMDR not all traumas need to be named for the therapy to be effective.

48. Van der Kolk, *Body Keeps the Score*, 255.

onto me, for I have not yet ascended to the Father" (John 20:17). Some translations say "do not touch" or "do not cling." The Greek word *haptou* is used throughout the biblical text to refer to a literal touch.[49] Jesus is telling Mary Magdalene, quite literally, not to touch him. This seems odd at first since he later invites Thomas to touch his wounds. Read with trauma in mind, however, the establishment of this boundary points to a healing of his invisible wounds. Having endured unconscionable suffering, Jesus now says who can touch him and when. In resurrection, love brings forth agency.

For survivors of incest, agency and appropriate boundaries are stolen at a young age, damaging future relationships with oneself and others.[50] Many survivors feel that in order to be loved they must acquiesce. Others may meet their relationships with aggression or abandonment, feeling ruled by their preprogrammed responses.[51] As persistent love is encountered and safety is discovered, survivors gain control of their bodies. In doing so, their voice, once silenced, is powerfully resurrected. Sexuality is reclaimed. Bodily autonomy is found. Power and agency are restored.[52]

Likewise, in resurrection, the betrayal felt by Jesus as his friends slept in the garden or denied him during his arrest is gently coated in the salve of belonging. The belief in a loving God that intervenes in situations of injustice is clarified as one is held in gentle affection by the hands of Christ at work in the world. As one's relationship with their embodied wounds transforms, grace and compassion naturally abound. When undertows of trauma are encountered throughout life, love enables the survivor to meet their experiences with compassion. It provides perspective, reminding one that occasional waves of flashbacks and intrusive memories are normal. The survivor is continually learning to walk in the resurrected life. One woman reminds us that "it is not a problem to be lost. It is only a problem if you think it is impossible to find your way home."[53]

The intrusive change brought about by the bodily resurrection of Christ and the encounter with love alters how one sees the wounds of trauma. It does not make them go away and it does not change the fact that horrible things occurred in childhood. It does not wash away the residue that survivors can still occasionally feel well into their "healed" life. It does,

49. Bible Hub, "Haptomi."

50. Allender, *Wounded Heart*, 89.

51. Allender, *Wounded Heart*, 158–70.

52. Shooter, *How Survivors of Abuse Relate to God*, 157.

53. Women of Magdalene and Stevens, *Find Your Way Home*, 45.

however, interrupt and reconstruct our lives in magnificent ways. It enables one to accept the unacceptable things that happened, moving one from a place of repression and denial to ownership and agency. In seeing wounds differently, one's identity is no longer dictated by the narrative of abuse. The wounds have their place in the larger narrative.

The resurrection of the crucified body tells a story unlike any other. Surpassing the limits of language, the body communicates a narrative replete with profound wisdom. Emanating from both visible and invisible wounds, the resurrected life offers a new way of knowing and experiencing the world. A transformed physicality harkens a return to the *imago Dei* and invites one to rest in the truth that sexual violence does not win. The innate wisdom of God shines forth from the sexually abused body, offering the persistent promise that not even the most horrific of abuses can keep one from knowing God. Just as the resurrected body of the crucified Christ tells a unique story of hope, so too does the body of each survivor. Unique to each person, but ultimately emanating the *imago Dei*, resurrected bodies tell of the wisdom gained through death, Holy Saturday, and new life. It is a wisdom about enduring pain, finding one's way, and radiating the power of love. It is the story of finding God in the unexpected place of the sexually abused body.

## RESURRECTION OF IDENTITY

> Being my body means living with a subjectivity that remains anchored in and bound to a prison constructed by another's permanent touch upon and within my flesh. I acknowledge such subjectivity to be a peculiar feature and torment of my life. Perhaps it is the only thing in this life I can honestly call mine.[54]

> For if we have been united with him in a death like his, we will certainly also be united with him in a resurrection like his. For we know that our old self was crucified with him so that the body ruled by sin might be done away with, that we should no longer be slaves to sin . . . . Now if we died with Christ, we believe that we will also live with him . . . . Therefore, do not let sin reign in your mortal body so that you obey its evil desires. Do not offer any part of yourself to sin as an instrument of wickedness, but rather offer

54. Grovijahn, "Feminist Theology of Survival," 18.

> yourselves to God as those who have been brought from death to life. (Rom 6:5–6, 6:8, 6:12–13)

The miracle of bodily resurrection is astounding. It is awe-inspiring not *just* for its miraculous occurrence, but also because of what it represents. It defies logic, offers hope in the face of oppression, and demonstrates an in-breaking of love that allows for spiritual transformation. In resurrection, life's most painful embodied memories are seen anew. In addition to all of this, however, resurrection also reshapes identity as one freed from the shackles of death. For Jesus and the survivor alike, this re-formation of identity is profound. In the aftermath of resurrection, the disciples finally understand who Jesus really is, and their misunderstanding falls away. God is seen. For survivors, resurrection offers the same hope—to see the self as God sees.

The re-formation of identity is built upon several historical theological changes that occurred in the aftermath of Christ's resurrection. N. T. Wright highlights these changes in his argument for a literal bodily resurrection.[55] He notes that prior to this event, first-century Judaism held non-specific and peripheral ideas regarding resurrection. Views of the afterlife existed on a spectrum, and people generally believed that resurrection would be a single, eschatological event that occurred at the end of time for all of God's people.[56] There was no clear or unified belief about what type of body resurrected people would have and, Wright argues, a middle-of-history resurrection experience (like that of Jesus) would seem preposterous.[57]

Jesus's death quickly moved resurrection to the focal point and clarified important details with rapid certainty.[58] In the new Christian movement this was a breakthrough event in history that called Christians to be active in the world, implementing the teachings of Jesus as they anticipated the final resurrection. This resurrection would be bodily. People would get a transformed body whose material, created from the old, would be incorruptible and incapable of decay and death.[59]

Reflection upon this experience brought with it new metaphors.[60] In Judaism, resurrection was commonly associated with the restoration of the

55. Wright, "Did Jesus Really Rise from the Dead?"

56. Wright, *Surprised by Hope*, 35–37.

57. Wright, *Surprised by Hope*, 39.

58. Wright, *Surprised by Hope*, 40; Wright, "Did Jesus Really Rise from the Dead?"

59. Wright, *Surprised by Hope*, 40.

60. Wright, *Surprised by Hope*, 45.

nation of Israel.[61] In Christianity, however, resurrection became a much more individualized and personal bodily experience. Baptism offered a ritual enactment of death and new life in association with Jesus. This is significant as the Jewish people anticipated a messiah who would overthrow oppressive rulers and take the throne as a literal Davidic king. No one would have expected a messiah to die and so no one would anticipate a resurrection.[62] The entire concept of "messiah" gets re-imagined in the Christian movement and, along with it, an understanding of how God operates in the world. With belief in the resurrection, a new and embodied life is made known in the aftermath. Death, the oppressor's greatest weapon, is destroyed. All this together supports society's transformed memory of who Jesus is. In resurrection, the wounded, triumphant, and vulnerable God is made known.

Without the resurrection narrative, Jesus was just another first-century prophet who espoused wise teachings.[63] The Gospel narratives themselves are proof that early Christians reflected on the personhood and resurrection of Jesus, with each Gospel painting a unique portrait of the Messiah. Jesus as the suffering servant in Mark, the Davidic teacher in Matthew, the prophetic savior in Luke, and the cosmic Christ in John are all informed by the belief in his defeat of death.[64] Predating these Gospels, the apostle Paul reflects on the bodily resurrection and personhood of Jesus, stating in 1 Corinthians, "Christ has indeed been raised from the dead . . . for since death came through a man, the resurrection of the dead comes also through a man. For as in Adam all die, so in Christ all will be made alive" (1 Cor 15:20–22). He goes on to state that "what you sow does not come to life unless it dies . . . so will it be with the resurrection of the dead. The body that is sown is perishable, it is raised imperishable, it is sown in dishonor, it is raised in glory; it is sown in weakness, it is raised in power" (1 Cor 15:36, 42–44).

William Hull notes that the appearance of the resurrected Christ marks the boundary of transition. His resurrection appearance "establish[es] the identity and continuity of the earthly Jesus with the risen Lord while at the same time defining the tremendous differences that resulted for the disciples in the shift."[65] In short, a transition occurs from "the seen to the

61. Wright, *Surprised by Hope*, 45.

62. Wright, *Surprised by Hope*, 45–47.

63. Wright, *Surprised by Hope*, 48; Wright, "Did Jesus Really Rise From the Dead?"

64. Strauss, *Four Portraits*.

65. Hull, "John," 367.

unseen, from the temporal to the eternal, from the limited to the universal, from the physical to the spiritual."[66] The resurrection offers the promise of transition from death to new life, from wounded to healed, from one defined by their greatest pains to one known by their victories.

This awareness of Jesus's identity creates space for reflection and reconnection. For early Christians, this meant understanding one's own identity in relationship to God and defining one's role in the world.[67] For survivors of incest, resurrection creates space for one to establish a new identity free from the bonds of trauma and see themselves as God sees them. It brings forth a new relationship with one's body and way of being in the world. Herman explains this new identity as reconnection:

> Having come to terms with the traumatic past, the survivor faces the task of creating a future. She has mourned the old self that the trauma destroyed; now she must develop a new self. Her relationships have been tested and forever changed by the trauma; now she must develop new relationships. The old beliefs that gave meaning to her life have been challenged; now she must find anew a sustaining faith . . . . In accomplishing this work, the survivor reclaims her world.[68]

In these transitions the survivor recognizes and understands the impact of her victimization all while incorporating this new wisdom into her life.[69] In this process old wounds are revisited. Whereas in the early stages of Holy Saturday one visited wounds from a defensive position, seeking to establish safety, now these wounds have lost their fierce sting.

Descending into the depths of hell and subsequently encountering love reawakens the *imago Dei* within the survivor. Memory is transformed as one encounters the knowledge that they are made in God's image. This resurrected wisdom is a glimmer of light pouring from the wound whose brightness grows under the gaze of awareness. Guilt and self-blame melt away in this light as the survivor realizes they no longer need to be "forgiven" for what happened to them. Grace pours into the cracks created by shame as the survivor breaks free from the lies of dehumanization. The body unapologetically takes up space, empowered with a sense of autonomy and connection.

66. Hull, "John," 367.

67. Wright, *Surprised by Hope*, 45; Crossan, "Jesus and the Challenge," 105–52.

68. Herman, *Trauma and Recovery*, 196.

69. Herman, *Trauma and Recovery*, 197.

An example of this is found in one survivor's description of reclaiming her sexuality and establishing a sense of safety in her intimate life. Having suffered from sadomasochistic fantasies, she made a conscious effort to rid herself of this pain.

> I came to the point where I really understood that they weren't *my* fantasies. They'd been imposed on me through abuse. And gradually, I began to have orgasms without thinking about the SM, without picturing my father doing something to me. Once I separated the fantasy from the feeling, I'd consciously impose other powerful images on that feeling—like seeing a waterfall. If they can put SM on you, you can put waterfalls there instead.[70]

In this instance, the memory is visited and revisited. As love breaks through, the pain that was inscribed in the body is overwritten. Both the bodily experience and identity formed within the bonds of trauma are made new. The wounds still exist in resurrection, but they no longer have the power to define and control.

Previously held captive by the chains of trauma, the survivor "no longer feels possessed by her traumatic past; she is in possession of herself."[71] Shame, guilt, and self-loathing, so often manifested as negative self-talk in the disguised voice of the abuser, are silenced as the survivor speaks her truth. In this phase, many feel a calling to disclose their stories, expose the family secret, and eradicate the rule of silence. By maintaining the family secret of abuse "they carry the weight of a burden that does not belong to them . . . they may choose to declare to their families that the rule of silence has been irrevocably broken."[72] Now the survivor is able to place the burden of guilt and shame where it belongs: on the abuser.[73] And while the family's response carries weight, the survivor has come to value and love themselves over and above the opinion of abusers. Freedom lies in finding a voice, breaking the silence, and proclaiming truth. One is now able to see the experience of silence with new eyes.

Having reflected not just on the abuse, but on how they survived, those in the midst of resurrection come to know themselves more deeply. Like it or not, the experience of incest forms aspects of one's character.[74] For

70. Herman, *Trauma and Recovery*, 203.

71. Herman, *Trauma and Recovery*, 202.

72. Herman, *Trauma and Recovery*, 200.

73. Herman, *Trauma and Recovery*, 200.

74. Crysdale, *Embracing Travail*, 20–25.

some, chaos and drama were integral parts of the childhood experience. As adults, they might find ways to perpetuate this cycle of chaos. Becoming aware of this and working to correct it free one from the bonds of death and create space to inhabit a new life. Similarly, another person might have found safety in dissociation. As an adult this may manifest in attempts to numb or ignore unpleasant experiences through self-medication.[75] In resurrection one is able to "recognize and 'let go'" of harmful character traits formed in the fires of trauma.

For a time, it is necessary to reflect on the trauma itself, which often leads to deep-seated theological questions about the abuse. Survival itself, however, is a theological act that can teach one about God.[76] Grovijahn notes that "survival actually reveals the power of Incarnation, making it real in history, operating as a manifestation of it."[77] The sexually abused body made in God's image functions as "the bridge between survival and Incarnation."[78] Living in the aftermath of incest requires leaning into pain, mystery, growth, discovery, joy, and love. Survival includes inhabiting a body that was once unsafe and feeling one's way through life. It is creative, imaginative, unintelligible, and formative for oneself and the surrounding world. It is, in short, revelatory of God.[79]

Walking in this light of resurrection, the survivor's imagination is reawakened. They are no longer dominated by repetitive traumatic memory and fantasy. Now, old dreams and new hopes converge.[80] As memories are healed, one's bodily autonomy is restored and the survivor gains a voice. One begins to realize that the damage done can be redeemed.[81] Doing so allows one to meet the darkest parts of themselves with acceptance and compassion. The survivor learns that the body holds both the experience of violation and the truth of the *imago Dei*. One survivor says:

> I am from chaos and confusion. I am from my father's lap, crawling down after he's passed out. I am from a pony bottle of Miller Genuine Draft. I am from a closet where I hid from my father. I am from a bathroom watching the blood from the needle shoot to the

75. Crysdale, *Embracing Travail*, 23.
76. Grovijahn, "Feminist Theology of Survival," 7.
77. Grovijahn, "Feminist Theology of Survival," 9.
78. Grovijahn, "Feminist Theology of Survival," 9.
79. Nelson, *Body Theology*, 50.
80. Herman, *Trauma and Recovery*, 202.
81. Crysdale, *Embracing Travail*, 95.

> ceiling. I am from a highway to hell on an early Saturday morning. I am from many schools. I am from dark alleys and early days. I am from my kids crawling out of my lap after I nodded out. I am from the smell of alcohol on many men. I am from addiction. I am from scorched Hamburger Helper that my babies had to eat. I am from March 13th, 2006. I am from a life of one to a life of many. I am from total darkness to pure light. I am from dying to recovering. I am from anger to forgiveness. I am from being nothing to being everything. I am from an addict in bondage to a recovering addict that's free.[82]

Both realities are held within the body: abuse and healing, addiction and recovery, disappointment and hope. Resurrection does not negate the passion nor does healing erase the memories of incest. Here the survivor boldly proclaims, "I am."

By awakening to the awareness that one's body knows death yet walks in life, a transformed physicality ensues.[83] Exposing one's identity to the light of resurrection allows one to see themselves as they are—loved and made in God's image. No longer is one a merely "victim" or "survivor" whose identity is wrapped up in trauma. Now one can come to see themselves as powerful, competent, loving, compassionate, creative, and ambitious. Mother, daughter, child, teacher, healer, caregiver, intellectual, change-maker, advocate, and other defining attributes have the space to move forward. Walking in the promise of new life, one gets to name for themselves how they want to be known. Wounds are transformed through encounters with persistent love. Torment is turned to consolation. Grace seeps into the dark crevices of one's mind and body, magnifying one's voice and one's being. Collateral beauty is discovered in the wreckage of trauma and peace prevails. Without the cloud of shame, one is free to be loved for exactly who they are. In resurrection the survivor comes to celebrate the fierce truth of the *imago Dei.*

## CONTINUAL RESURRECTION

Although the narrative of Christ's death, descent, and resurrection offers a powerful metaphor for survivors of incest, the path to resurrection is not linear. Indeed, one will become aware of deaths endured intermittently

82. Women of Magdalene and Stevens, *Find Your Way Home*, 52.

83. Wright, *Surprised by Hope*, 44.

throughout life. The descent into hell will happen again and again as one embarks on the holy work of healing. Resurrection, too, will be encountered more than once. It is, perhaps, more accurate to say that the survivor will encounter several mini resurrections over the course of a lifetime, each one bringing them closer to the truth of God's love.

Healing does not happen all at once. It sometimes feels fragmented and disjointed. It can be awkward as one learns to re-inhabit the body. Stiff from the confines of the grave, resurrection can feel like the joy of a good-morning stretch. It is waking up to a world of possibility. As one's creative imagination turns away from the horrors of trauma, the body is cleansed with a glimmer of light that emerges from the site of suffering, illuminating the *imago Dei*.[84]

Learning to recognize and honor that one is made in God's image is a journey. Incest survivors have been taught that they are not deserving of love and often grow through life feeling broken, ashamed, and dirty. Embracing the truth of the *imago Dei* is holy work. It is God's call to us as survivors. Daily, as one makes efforts to pay attention to the body and all that it can teach, one must discover ways to care for and celebrate the body. Resurrected with wounds, living and leading with the knowledge of death, creating narratives from broken pieces—the survivor experience is a kaleidoscope of magnificent beauty.

The body marked by incest, made small and insignificant in the abusive home, unapologetically takes up space in the resurrected life. Repeatedly convinced that they are a problem and burden, the body and being proudly proclaims healing and solutions to suffering in a broken world. As the survivor steps into this new identity, one learns to honor the body instead of abusing it, to give voice to the body instead of silencing it, and to meet the body with the light of love instead of the darkness of shame. Once a place to merely escape, now one seeks to connect and fully inhabit the body.

The experience of child sexual abuse in the form of incest will always be part of our stories, just as the crucifixion is part of Jesus's. In the Last Supper, he instructs his disciples to think of his body, broken and bleeding, as they partake of the bread and wine. Death and brokenness, however, are not the end. The resurrection gives new meaning to the entire narrative. As each survivor becomes whom God has called them to be, stories will undoubtedly be transformed. Trauma is no longer the defining factor of one's life. Beneath it all is the enduring, beautiful truth that we are made in God's image.

84. See chapter 5.

# 7
# Conclusion

*In the trenches of abuse, I stand*
*Insistent on the power of healing,*

*Mirroring the way marbled with hard-won wisdom*
*Mystically knowing the purpose which God has given me.*

*As I authoritatively demonstrate the power of new life*
*And adventurously advocate for the teaching of the good news,*

*God's hope and plan are made known as grace governs me.*
*Graciously growing through the Great Commission,*

*Opening my heart to the presence of others like me as my story*
*Operates as an offering on the altar of Christ.*

*Demanding delivery of justice I am called to*
*De-mystify the crucified pain of incest,*

*Exceed expectations of healing and*
*Exalt stories of the victimized, surviving, thriving Children of God.*

*Immersed and immersing others in love*
*Inviting all into a safe and welcoming community of the*
*imago Dei.*

Child sexual abuse in the form of incest is a trauma so severe, all-consuming, and horrendous, that it has been likened to death. It is a trauma that persists long after its initial occurrence and infiltrates the expanse of time. The effects of incest live in the body, malforming one's sense of self and convincing the child that they are inherently bad and shameful. Deicide, or the death of how one knows God, occurs as the child's innocent body is pierced, pillaged, and crucified by sexual violation.

Despite this harm, God is made known through the sexually violated body. This research has examined the experience of incest through a theological lens, paying close attention to the body and the *imago Dei*. Survivors learn to live in bodies marked by violations that seemingly alter one's very being. Despite this, it is possible to encounter God through the body. The narrative of Jesus illuminates the path of resurrection and offers the promise of embodying an impossible love that has the power to transform both individuals and communities. This concluding chapter will summarize the key points of this research, highlight the contributions and limitations of this study, and note areas for further exploration.

## SUMMARY

The first half of this work contextualizes the experience of incest and provides a theological framework for understanding the spiritual wound that it inflicts. In chapter 1, the prevalence and bio-psycho-social impact of incest is outlined. It is noted that approximately one in four girls will be sexually abused before the age of eighteen, and most abuse occurs at the hands of a family member or close acquaintance. Sexual violation is but one aspect of the abuse, and it is often accompanied by a dysfunctional home environment. Loss of safety, neglect, violence, chaos, and domineering or cold parental figures all typically accompany experiences of incest. Societal structures contribute to this harm as children are often blamed, attacked, or outright ignored. This harm is compounded over time and the child embodies this violation and oppression. As a result, victims of incest experience long-term negative health outcomes including an increased risk of cancer, cardiovascular disease, auto-immune disorders, mood disorders, addiction, anxiety, and suicide.

This embodied harm extends into the realm of identity and faith development. Utilizing the fields of transpersonal and developmental psychology, chapter 2 of this work explores how a child's God-image is formed.

Both self-image and God-image are constructed in dynamic and complex ways, born from a sense of belonging and safety in infancy. In other words, how one understands self and God is shaped by one's primary caregivers. A child's relationship with their parents is thus spiritually formative. As a child's sense of self and faith develops, they are heavily informed by how they *think* God (and their parents) see them. For the survivor of incest, this directly impacts the belief that they are made in God's image.

Although the concept of the *imago Dei* has historically been understood in a multitude of ways, as outlined and discussed in chapter 2, it is nevertheless through the body that one comes to know and experience God. For the incest survivor, it is through the *sexually abused* body that God is made known. As a result of harm and violation, one's God-image becomes layered with the dysfunction and loss of safety present in the home. The body becomes a place of suffering and oppression as violating touch lingers within the skin. Incest attacks the core of who one is and teaches the child that they are not a person before God. In short, this violation leads to a deicide or death of how one knows God.

So how is it possible to access the truth of God's love in a body that has been brutalized by another's violating touch? Alongside unspeakable memories of violation, the body also holds remarkable wisdom. Chapter 3 of this work explores this wisdom through the lens of embodied theology by examining the social location of the sexually abused body, exploring how the lived experience shapes human theological knowing and looking to the body of God as an example. While incest is the point of deicide, it is also the starting point for divine revelation. It demands divine justice and reveals the divine capacity to heal from ineffable wounds.

The second half of this work turns to the Christ narrative to demonstrate these truths. Drawing upon David Tracy's *Analogical Imagination*, chapters 4, 5, and 6 explore Good Friday, Holy Saturday, and Easter Sunday in conjunction with the experience of incest. Although comparing the experience of Jesus to that of incest survivors is not an exact metaphor, it nevertheless provides space to deeply discuss the spiritual wounds inflicted. New insights emerge when reading from a hermeneutic of rape, which can facilitate theological reflection throughout the healing journey.

In chapter 4, it is argued that Christ encounters a myriad of deaths on the way to his crucifixion. He experiences a death of safety, innocence, and the body as he is betrayed, sexually abused, and crucified. Abandoned in the Garden of Gethsemane, betrayed by Judas, and denied by Peter, Jesus, like the incest survivor, embodies a loss of safety as his torment looms nearby. His public stripping and humiliation are forms of sexual abuse intended to shame and dehumanize. Just as incest survivors are often silenced, this sexually abusive experience of Jesus is also commonly ignored in the passion narratives. His body is ultimately crucified. As he hangs on the cross and his body bears the weight of death, the very notion of who God is becomes challenged. The expectations that others had of his identity are altered.

Holy Saturday, the day between death and resurrection, is a liminal space marked by ambiguity, mystery, and transformation. On this day, Jesus descended into hell and forged a path across the chasm. There is no clear doctrine outlining the specifics. Many are eager to bypass it altogether and focus instead on resurrection. However, learning to remain in this mystery is preeminently important on the journey. It is in this space of liminality that the survivor gains coping mechanisms, pieces together their narrative, and confronts the darkness of hell. It is also here that one discovers the bridge that leads to light and new life. It is out of one's wounds that a trickle of divine love emerges.

Emerging from the depths of hell, Jesus is resurrected on the third day. He encounters Mary Magdalene at the tomb and, although the details vary within the Gospel accounts, he meets the disciples in their fear and grief. Once dead and now alive, he appears with his wounds. Disbelief, fear, and awe abound as Jesus invites them to inspect his hands and feet. They touch his side and know him by his broken body. They break bread with him, drink with him, and converse with him. Resurrection shipwrecks their ordinary way of knowing and demands a shift in consciousness. Now, in the wake of their risen teacher, they must *be* and *know* differently in the world. Reflecting on new life while embodying death results in a revaluation of the body and identity. It is through persistent encounters with love that this emergence into new life is made possible.

The wounds accrued through incest are embodied, shaping how one comes to understand self, God, and themselves in relation to God. As with Jesus, the wounds remain, but in this phase of life they have their place in the larger narrative. The sexually abused body reveals God and points one to the truth of the *imago Dei*. In reconnecting with the body, one learns that it holds both death and life, oppression and freedom, and darkness and light. Resurrection is not merely the therapeutic experience of "healing." It is a profound spiritual transformation that liberates one from the chains of death. It is the process by which one comes to see themselves as God sees them: loved and made in God's image.

## CONTRIBUTIONS

Healing is made possible through encounters with safety and love, but the burden of healing cannot and should not be placed upon the survivor alone. This work speaks not only to survivors of incest but also to those who journey with us. It is a call to the church, society, and academy to think more deeply and sit more intently with those who have endured such atrocities. Then, and only then, can others operate as the hands and feet of Christ to meet the needs of the sexually abused.

In the Gospel texts, the resurrection is made known through the witness of others. The disciples, having traveled with Jesus throughout his ministry, witnessed great miracles. They saw him heal people, feed people, and love people in radical counter-cultural ways. They also saw him die and live again. Their encounter was so mind boggling and astonishing that it demanded a new way of being in the world. Wright describes the resurrected Jesus as having a "transformed physicality." Upon his reappearance, it becomes evident that he is somehow *different.* Jesus is "a firmly embodied human being whose body possesses new, unexpected, and unexplained characteristics."[1] He is the same person, inhabiting the same body, and yet, there is something fundamentally different about him. Didymus of Alexandria says, "somehow, then, what is raised is both other than and the same as the body that perishes."[2] He is no longer recognizable as a victim. Power pours from his wounds. As a result, the disciples are willing to risk their lives and challenge the world as they know it to spread the good news of his teachings and resurrection.

Although details across the Gospels differ slightly, all are consistent in the fact that Mary Magdalene is among the first to encounter the resurrected Jesus.[3] In the patriarchal biblical world it is interesting that Mary, a woman, is the first to meet him. Historically Mary is often inaccurately and unfairly cast as a sinner guilty of sexual indiscretion.[4] According to Luke 8:2 Jesus casts seven demons out of her. Her healing is set apart from others, but not much detail is given. It is likely that she suffered from some type of psychic disorder that affected her physically and mentally. An ailment not

1. Wright, *Resurrection of the Son of God*, 661.
2. Kovacs, *1 Corinthians Interpreted*, 110.
3. Ricci, *Mary Magdalene*, 139.
4. Ricci, *Mary Magdalene*, 150.

easily understood and therefore categorized as demonic possession, one can assume that Mary was "dispossessed of herself."[5]

Theologian Carla Ricci notes that upon her healing she "came back from Jesus as a woman restored to herself, to the depths of her own being. And perhaps rather than one central moment, there was a process, a developing relationship of discovery and growth."[6] A close companion of her healer, Mary grieved deeply at Jesus's death. In all the Gospel accounts, she is a witness to the crucifixion, and she visits the tomb early after Sabbath. Her grief is an outpouring of love. When she discovers his body is missing, she alerts the others and then stays to weep. Desperately looking for the one who brought her back to herself, she asks the gardener to take her to his body.

> Her whole being is bent on finding him. And Jesus allows himself to be found, lets himself be recognized. He says her name, "Mary!" . . . in hearing herself called, the woman finds at the same time the voice she knows, the voice of the other, and now here the Other, and finds herself, her perception and understanding of her own depths.[7]

Stated differently, by encountering the resurrected Christ this healed woman also discovers herself.

Why is it Mary Magdalene to whom the resurrected Christ first appears? Is it the trauma of her demonic possession, the experience of feeling lost in her own mind and body, that gives her the ability to see the wounded and living Christ before others? Is it her persistence to be close to God despite her pain? Perhaps it is the social location of her female body, the unlikely messenger in a patriarchal society, that makes her the ideal candidate to tell others the good news of Christ's radical love. She recognizes Jesus when he says her name. She tells the disciples, "I have seen the Lord!" (John 20:18).

The message that Mary receives from both angelic messengers and Christ himself is "do not be afraid" and "go tell the disciples." This first commission provides the foundation for the birth of the church. She is the first apostle. What an empowering truth for the survivor of sexual violence! A woman historically known for sexual sins knows about Christ's resurrection before all others. Do not be afraid! Go tell! It is this commission

5. Ricci, *Mary Magdalene*, 137.

6. Ricci, *Mary Magdalene*, 138.

7. Ricci, *Mary Magdalene*, 143.

that so many survivors are living out in the resurrected life. In the wake of movements like #MeToo so many are overcoming their fear and speaking the truth. By doing so they are living out the gospel, following Christ's commands, and changing the world.

The ultimate question following this is simple: How will the followers of Christ respond? The Gospel of Luke says, "They did not believe the women, because their words seemed to them like nonsense. Peter, however, got up and ran to the tomb" (Luke 24:11–12). Will the church listen as abused women speak their truth? Will they run to the tomb in disbelief? Or will they seek Jesus in an effort to create a more loving world? When Jesus appears to his disciples in the Gospel of Matthew, he issues the Great Commission: "All authority in heaven and on earth has been given to me. Therefore go and make disciples of all nations, baptizing them in the name of the Father and of the Son and of the Holy Spirit, and teaching them to obey everything I have commanded you. And surely I am with you always, to the very end of the age" (Matt 28:18–20). In this command, his people are to spread the good news of love and salvation to all people. As Jesus ascends, Christians are to be his hands and feet in the world, operating as the body of Christ.

This Great Commission brings with it the task of redefining love for a broken world. The love put forth by the gospel is one that celebrates survivors of incest as people made in God's image. It is not conditional or coercive. It is a love that respects one's inherent dignity, celebrates one's gifts, and immerses the survivor in grace. It is a love that celebrates truth. Fueled by this love, survivors of incest emerging into a resurrected life find the courage and creativity to experience life in new ways. To do so means embracing life with the wisdom of a sexually abused body. Is it possible for one to have a child of their own and safeguard them from abuse? Can one experience sex and intimacy steeped in love and equality rather than control and oppression? Can a survivor learn to love and fully live in their body, celebrating its goodness each day? After the pain of sexual violation and deicide, can one come to know God within the sexually violated body? The answer, of course, is yes.

The commission to the disciples is to spread the good news of love and encourage others to obey the teachings of Christ. Institutions such as the church must live out this call in a sexually traumatized world. One of the easiest and most profound things a community can do is return to the body. Grovijahn notes that we have "spiritualized [the] reality of *imago Dei* right out of the flesh."[8] So often in worship the body is discussed only in relation to sin and desire. For an incest survivor whose embodied experience is excruciating, this message only makes recovery more difficult. What if the body was discussed as the miracle that it is? It is through the body, with all its experiences, that one knows God. It is a new life with wounds that offers hope. The survivor's body points to the miracle of Incarnation, to the persistence of God's creativity, love, and power within our broken world.[9] To embrace embodiment in worship would be a powerful thing.

Realizing the realities of abuse is the first step on this path toward embodied knowing. For church leaders, this means acknowledging that there are sexual abuse survivors within the congregation and community who likely suffer from the long-term impacts wrought by such abuse. Statistics and numbers translate to real people in real communities. Approximately 25 percent of women in any given congregation know the burden of abuse. Acknowledging this reality can have a transformative impact. For example, one pastor who was herself a victim of child sexual abuse preached for six to eight weeks on abuse. Sadler notes:

> Since that time—now this is a church of eighty people—she's had twenty-five women from the ages of sixty-five to eighty-five come forward and tell her that they are survivors of either childhood sexual abuse or adult sexual assault. Half of those women had never shared anything about that before until they told her. One of them was an eighty-five-year-old woman. Think about this. Think about an eighty-five-year-old woman, a woman who has spent most of her life in the church, and has never, until she's eighty-five years old, felt safe enough to come forward and share that.[10]

Having the courage to discuss sexual violence within the church can bring forth healing in ways that one cannot even imagine.

In order to foster such conversation, however, communities must be willing to listen and educate themselves on the experience of incest and sexual violence. Making an effort to connect with survivors and honor their stories is a powerful starting point. It is with wisdom that survivors speak their truth and boldly inhabit bodies freed from oppression. These children of God are all too familiar with suffering and spiritual pain. Who better

8. Grovijahn, "Theology as an Irruption," 35.

9. Grovijahn, "Theology as an Irruption," 7.

10. Sadler, *Vulnerability*, 126.

to lead others through the darkness?[11] Survivor-leaders are invaluable resources within communities. They are not mere recipients of ministry. Like Mary Magdalene, they are apostles called to inform others of the joy of resurrection.

Communities can empower survivor-leaders in several ways. For example, one might establish an advisory board to rethink issues of trauma in worship. Survivors of trauma who have done the difficult work of healing would provide excellent and meaningful input in such an endeavor. Alternatively, small groups and/or Bible studies led by survivors can also enrich individuals and the community. One might choose to lead yoga or contemplative prayer each week to gently reconnect with both God and the body. Many survivors, however, do not wish to be known by their experience of trauma. It is preeminently important that communities create safe spaces to allow one to come forward if they so desire, but also simply celebrate people for who they are and the unique gifts they embody. Encouraging community involvement and allowing one to find purpose in their own gifts is a profound method of empowerment. In doing so, individual purpose is discovered, and the whole community is enhanced.

In addition to lifting up survivor leaders, this work also calls on communities to read relevant literature, educate communities, make local healing resources available, and study religious texts from a hermeneutic of rape. Community education can occur via sermons, informational pamphlets, or even short surveys which collect data regarding how congregations currently understand trauma. As each of these is implemented, the community can grow in deeper understanding. Normalizing discussion surrounding trauma contributes to the construction of a safe space and meets sexually traumatized people in their pain.

From this, communities are encouraged to reflect on and revise liturgy to be more trauma informed.[12] Such reflection might include reconsideration of hymns that may have obvious triggering language or inviting rather than commanding individuals to participate in rituals. For example, "I now invite you to" rather than "now we will" gives freedom of choice. Additionally, litanies can be included which emphasize concepts such as the body,

11. Shooter, *How Survivors of Abuse Relate to God*, 170–71.

12. Monica Coleman's work *The Dinah Project* is an exceptional guidebook for congregations seeking to become more trauma-informed. The appendices in the work provide ready-made templates for religious communities and range in content from educational resources, to recruitment letters, to liturgy. Coleman, *Dinah Project*.

healing, struggles, and affirmations.[13] One might even offer special services focused on healing from sexual violence. Such services would ideally have contact information for additional resources readily available. Several options for local counseling, community support, and online resources should be slipped into every program or made available by the door.

For the incest survivor who lives while embodying death there is, however, nothing more important in the healing journey than discovering safety and love within the body. Over time, oppressive violation and movement of the body have taught painful lies of degradation. Coleman notes that "the church is called to give the kind of response that legal, psychological, and medical personnel do not and cannot give."[14] The church can help one embrace positive, healing, soulful movement in a body in ways which bring forth life. Simply paying attention to what physical bodies are doing during worship can have a significant impact.

For example, to seek salvation in many Evangelical Protestant churches one must make a public confession, kneel at the altar, and recite the sinner's prayer. Phrased another way, the incest survivor must get on their knees (sometimes at the feet of a male pastor), be touched involuntarily, and state that they are a sinner. What has the trauma survivor's body learned in the movement of kneeling, being touched, and feeling a sense of uncleanliness? To gain access to God one must carry out rhythmic movements which were enacted during the traumatic event. While taking the steps to the altar is voluntary, the avenue through which one finds salvation is restricted. Kneeling at the feet of a pastor, usually a man, to deliver a prayer regarding uncleanliness and sin can be triggering, shameful, and humiliating—the exact opposite of what is intended in the ritual.

Rethinking ritual from a trauma-informed perspective requires an intentional connection with the body. It demands an acknowledgment that our bodies are storehouses of memory and brings forth gratitude for our embodied encounters with God. Putting the body back in worship can be as simple as a short body-scan meditation or as involved as a sermon series on the goodness of the body. Whatever steps are taken, it is with the intention of helping bodies learn safety and love. Paulo Coelho notes that "when we love, we always strive to become better than we are [and] everything around us becomes better too."[15]

13. Coleman, *Dinah Project*, 122–23.

14. Coleman, *Dinah Project*, 5.

15. Coelho, *Alchemist*, 155.

Resurrecting experiences of safety and love within the body results in an outpouring of light. The Great Commission naturally emerges as one feels *called* to share the good news with others. For some survivors of incest, this calling manifests in very literal and concrete ways. Herman notes:

> Most survivors seek the resolution of their traumatic experience within the confines of their personal lives. But a significant minority, as a result of the trauma, feel called upon to engage in a wider world . . . . While there is no way to compensate for an atrocity, there is a way to transcend it, by making it a gift to others.[16]

Social action magnifies one's wisdom and capacities while offering connection with others. Herman states, "It brings out the best in her; in return, the survivor gains a sense of connection with the best in other people."[17] This social action can take many forms and connects one to the reality that there are a multitude of other people on this journey. Many have not found their way to a safe space and are still being brutalized. Others are living out their lives hidden in plain sight. Moving forward in solidarity with other survivors is a manifestation of this compassion, reconnecting the survivor with the community.

For most, however, this calling is made known in everyday actions such as sharing a meal or exercising with a friend. In ordinary life, one uses the wisdom gained to communicate the importance of love and grace throughout life's journey. This calling is no less important. Margaret Mead is famous for saying, "Never doubt that a small group of thoughtful committed individuals can change the world. In fact, it's the only thing that ever has."[18] Creating a safe and loving space is, ultimately, the path laid out before us by Jesus. It is the gospel.

It is through this reflection, continual conversation, witness, and discernment that communities grow together to become empowering environments for traumatized people. It is in this way that the body of Christ combats the evils of incest. The preeminent contribution of this work is to shine a light on the dark shame of incest. The spiritual wounds inflicted by such experiences do not disqualify one from a life of joy and salvation. The destruction wrought becomes a seedbed for a new life, allowing divine love to spring forth in wild, unpredictable, radical ways. It is my great hope

16. Herman, *Trauma and Recovery*, 207.

17. Herman, *Trauma and Recovery*, 207–8.

18. As quoted in Shapiro, *New Yale Book of Quotations*, 542.

that the witness of this work will be the hands and feet of God in a sexually traumatized world.

## LIMITATIONS AND FURTHER RESEARCH

This work has gazed at a complex problem with a broad lens. The value in such a long, loving gaze lies in seeing the larger picture. In the case of incest, a topic that is taboo and avoided, this long gaze helps one grasp the magnitude of pain involved and realize the spiritual wounds inflicted. The intention of this work has not been to overturn every stone and explore every conversation. Rather, it has been to offer an entry point for Christian survivors and communities to grow and heal together.

The limitations throughout are also points of growth and further research. For example, the context in which incest is made possible is presented in this work from the perspective of Western culture. It is limited in global scope and does not take into account the dynamics at play in different cultures and systems. One such area of growth would be a more comparative, global, and contextual understanding of the experience of incest within specific communities.

As such, this work also does not include insights from comparative religions. Eastern understandings and approaches to suffering, for example, differ greatly from Western psychological understandings. Intentionally examining resources such as Asian-feminist approaches or socially engaged Buddhist approaches would provide alternative angles to understanding the theological problem of incest.

This work is composite in nature, drawing largely upon previously published narratives of incest survivors. It would be greatly strengthened by participant interviews and focus groups. While studies examining the impact of abuse on God-image have been utilized here, talking specifically to incest survivors about their experience in relation to the Christ narrative would serve to deepen and enrich the theological premises put forth. Additionally, interviews and focus groups could establish a safe and loving community, creating space to study the theological premises set forth in this work.

As stated in the preface, this research is personal and therefore is written with an inherent bias. Much of this academic work speaks to my own spiritual journey and is, in many ways, autoethnographic. The gift in this approach is a deep understanding of the experience of incest and the journey toward healing, as well as an invitation for the reader to become transformed by the narrative. Some may consider this narrative approach limiting as it is neither objective nor quantifiable.

These limitations, among others, offer avenues for further exploration. Some areas of this work are rich with possibility and brimming with necessity. For example, this work does not discuss forgiveness, sin, or evil at any length. Does a survivor need to forgive their abuser in order to heal? If everyone is made in God's image, then how does one reconcile the fact that the abuser is also in this image? How does one reconcile anger with God? The questions wrought during Holy Saturday are not contained in a neat space or time in life. They merit further consideration at every stage of the journey.

One of the most inexplicable questions that remains is "Why me?" Why does one survivor find a path of resurrection and unending support while another lives a life of addiction that ends in death? Why is one child saved from incest while so many more endure violation night after night? Where is God in the injustice of those still caught in the throes of sexual torment? Perhaps this is the preeminent call of this work. It is the commission to love the sexually abused. It is God's grace that breaks through to equip people and societies with the ability to be the hands and feet of Christ.

The task of theology is to make known the grace and incarnation of God.[19] Although mysterious and leaving unanswerable questions in its wake, grace makes known the love of God and the continuing incarnation of Christ. The insights outlined in this work and those to come are a result of cooperating with such grace. Crysdale notes that "in any insight, any discovery, there is a certain lack of control, a certain patience required . . . once we have an insight, our consciousness shifts in some irreversible way."[20] It is by cooperating with and positioning ourselves for these insights that we accept this grace and trust in its power to change the world.[21]

## CONCLUSION

The journey from deicide to resurrection is not linear. It is full of twists and turns, undertows, and waves, many of which leave survivors feeling bereft and adrift in their pain. As survivors embody an ongoing death, the God

19. Kelly, *Karl Rahner*, 343.
20. Crysdale, *Embracing Travail*, 37.
21. Crysdale, *Embracing Travail*, 38.

question endures. Looking to Christ provides an analogy through which the experience of one's deepest pains and most authentic life can be known. At the outset of this work it was asked, "In the aftermath of childhood sexual abuse that shakes and seemingly alters the substance of one's being, how is it even possible to know, build a relationship with, or access the truth of God's love?"

It is through the sexually violated body that God is made known. It is from one's wounds that a trickle of divine light flows, harkening one back to the very substance of who we are. God is found in the muck. God persists in the violation. Betrayed, abandoned, sexually abused, degraded, and destroyed, Jesus wept and then descended into hell, only to emerge anew. Walking with a transformed physicality, he commissioned others to spread a message of love replete with his wounds. As survivors of incest find voice and claim dignity, God commands Christians to create a world in which responsibility is shared. No longer does the survivor need to shoulder the weight of abuse alone. As grace breaks through, survivors and those journeying alongside are called to cooperate deeply and intentionally with the divine power of healing. May all survivors live in the knowledge of love. Embody the truth that you are made in God's image.

# Bibliography

Aalders, G. C. *Genesis*. Vol. 2. Grand Rapids: Zondervan, 1981.
Alexander, Jeffrey. *Trauma: A Social Theory*. Cambridge: Polity, 2012.
Allen, P. *The Concept of Woman*. Vol. 2. Grand Rapids: Eerdmans, 2002.
Allender, Dan. *The Wounded Heart: Hope for Adult Victims of Childhood Sexual Abuse*. Colorado Springs: NavPress, 1990.
Althaus, P. *The Theology of Martin Luther*. Philadelphia: Fortress, 1966.
American Psychiatric Association. *Desk Reference to the Diagnostic Criteria from DSM-5*. Arlington, VA: American Psychiatric Association, 2013.
Anderson, A. A. *2 Samuel*. Word Biblical Commentary 11. Dallas: Word Books, 1998.
Augustine. *City of God*. Translated by Marcus Dods. In Nicene and Post-Nicene Fathers, First Series, Vol. 2. Edited by Philip Schaff. Buffalo, NY: Christian Literature, 1887. Revised and edited by Kevin Knight. https://www.newadvent.org/fathers/1201.htm.
———. *Confessions*. Translated by R. S. Pine-Coffin. London: Penguin, 1961.
———. *De Trinitate*. Patrologia Latina 42. Edited by J. P. Migne. https://patristica.net/latina/#t042.
———. *St Augustine: On the Holy Trinity; Doctrinal Treatises; Moral Treatises*. Post-Nicene Fathers. Edited by Philip Schaff. Grand Rapids: Eerdmans, 2004.
Baldwin, Jennifer. *Trauma Sensitive Theology: Thinking Theologically in the Era of Trauma*. Eugene, OR: Wipf and Stock, 2018.
Balthasar, Hans Urs von. *First Glance at Adrienne von Speyr*. San Francisco: Ignatius, 1981.
———. *Heart of the World*. San Francisco: Ignatius, 1979.
———. *My Work: In Retrospect*. San Francisco: Ignatius, 1993.
———. *Science, Religion, and Christianity*. Translated by Hilda Graef. London: Burns and Oates, 1958.
———. *You Crown the Year with Your Goodness: Sermons Through the Liturgical Year*. Translated by Graham Harrison. San Francisco: Ignatius, 1989. Kindle.
Barr, Beth Allison. *The Making of Biblical Womanhood: How the Subjugation of Women Became Gospel Truth*. Grand Rapids: Brazos, 2021.
Barr, James. "The Image of God and Natural Theology." In *Biblical Faith and Natural Theology: The Gifford Lectures for 1991*, 156–73. Oxford: Clarendon, 1993.
Barth, Karl. *Church Dogmatics*. Vol. 3/2: *The Doctrine of Creation*. Edited by G. W. Bromiley and T. F. Torrance. Edinburgh: T & T Clark, 1960.
Bechtel, Lyn M. "What If Dinah Is Not Raped? (Genesis 34)." *Journal for the Study of the Old Testament* 62 (1994) 19–36.

Bender, L., and A. Blau. "The Reaction of Children to Sexual Relations with Adults." *American Journal of Orthopsychiatry* 7 (1937) 500–518.

Beonio-Brocchieri, M. T. "The Feminine Mind in Medieval Mysticism." In *Creative Women in Medieval and Early Modern Italy*, edited by A. Matter and J. Coakley, 19–33. Philadelphia: University of Pennsylvania Press, 1994.

Best, Jonathan. "Liminality and Perhaps." *Liminality Project* (blog), Jan. 31, 2020. https://www.theliminalityproject.org/2020/01/31/liminality-jonathan-best/.

Bible Hub. "680. Haptomi." https://biblehub.com/greek/680.htm.

Birky, I., and S. Ball. "Parental Trait Influence on God as an Object Representation." *Journal of Psychology* 122 (1987) 133–37.

Blumenthal, Henry J., and A. Hilary Armstrong. "Platonism." *Encyclopaedia Britannica Online*, May 22, 2020. https://www.britannica.com/topic/Platonism.

Brakke, David. *The Gnostics: Myth, Ritual, and Diversity in Early Christianity*. Cambridge, MA: Harvard University Press, 2010.

Briere, John, and Catherine Scott. *Principles of Trauma Therapy: A Guide to Symptoms, Evaluation, and Treatment*. London: Sage, 2006.

Brown, Peter. *Augustine of Hippo: A Biography*. Berkeley: University of California Press, 2000.

Brown, Raymond E. *Death of the Messiah*. New York: Doubleday, 1994.

Brueggemann, Walter. *Cadences of Home: Preaching Among Exiles*. Louisville: Westminster John Knox, 1997.

———. *Genesis*. Interpretation. Atlanta: John Knox, 1982.

Bruteau, Beatrice. "The Great Sabbath." *New Blackfriars* 71 (1990) 132–40.

Butler, Judith. *Gender Trouble: Feminism and the Subversion of Identity*. New York: Routledge, 1990.

Byrd, Aimee. *Recovering Biblical Manhood and Womanhood: How the Church Needs to Rediscover Her Purpose*. Grand Rapids: Zondervan, 2020.

Cahill, Lisa Sowle. *Sex, Gender, and Christian Ethics*. New York: Cambridge University Press, 1996.

Cairns, D. *The Image of God in Man*. London: Collins, 1953.

Calvin, John. *The Institutes of the Christian Religion*. Edited by J. T. McNeill. Philadelphia: Westminster, 1960.

Carmichael, Calum. *Women, Law, and the Genesis Traditions*. Edinburgh: Edinburgh University Press, 1979.

*Catechism of the Catholic Church*. 2nd ed. Washington, DC: United States Catholic Conference, 1997.

Clines, D. J. A. "The Image of God in Man." *Tyndale Bulletin* 19 (1968) 54–61.

Coats, George. *Genesis with an Introduction to Narrative Literature*. Vol. 1, *The Forms of Old Testament Literature*. Edited by Rolf Knierim and Gene M. Tucker. Grand Rapids: Eerdmans, 1983.

Coelho, Paulo. *The Alchemist*. 25th anniversary ed. Translated by Alan R. Clarke. New York: HarperOne, 2014.

Coleman, Monica. *The Dinah Project: A Handbook for Congregational Response to Sexual Violence*. Eugene, OR: Wipf & Stock, 2004.

Collins, A. O. "Purity." In *Mercer Dictionary of the Bible*, edited by Watson Mills, 725. Macon, GA: Mercer University Press, 1990.

Cone, James. *The Cross and the Lynching Tree*. Maryknoll, NY: Orbis, 2011.

Conley, C. "Rape and Justice in Victorian England." *Victorian Studies* 29 (1986) 519–36.

Cooey, Paula. *Religious Imagination and the Body: A Feminist Analysis*. New York: Oxford University Press, 1994.

Cooper-White, Pamela. *The Cry of Tamar: Violence Against Women and the Church's Response*. Minneapolis: Fortress, 2012.

Copeland, M. Shawn. *Enfleshing Freedom: Body, Race, and Being*. Minneapolis: Fortress, 2010.

Courtois, Christine. "Healing the Incest Wound: A Treatment Update with Attention to Recovered Memory Issues." *American Journal of Psychotherapy* 51 (1997) 464–96.

Creamer, Deborah Beth. *Disability and Christian Theology: Embodied Limits and Constructive Possibilities*. New York: Oxford University Press, 2009.

Crisp, Beth. "Reading Scripture from a Hermeneutic of Rape." *Theology and Sexuality* 14 (2001) 23–42.

Crossan, John Dominic. *Jesus: A Revolutionary Biography—A Startling Account of What We Can Know About the Life of Jesus*. San Francisco: HarperCollins, 1994.

———. "Jesus and the Challenge of Collaborative Eschatology." In *The Historical Jesus: Five Views*, edited by James J. Beilby and Paul Rhodes Eddy, 105–52. Downers Grove, IL: InterVarsity, 2009.

Crysdale, Cynthia. *Embracing Travail: Retrieving the Cross Today*. New York: Continuum, 2001.

Culpepper, R. Alan. "Luke." In *Luke–John*, edited by Leander Keck, 1–490. The New Interpreter's Bible 9. Nashville: Abingdon, 1995.

Daly, Mary. *Beyond God the Father: Toward a Philosophy of Women's Liberation*. Boston: Beacon, 1973.

———. *The Church and the Second Sex*. Boston: Beacon, 1968.

Damis, Louis F. "The Role of Implicit Memory in the Development and Recovery of Trauma-Related Disorders." *NeuroSci* 3 (2022) 63–88.

Da Silva, Chantal. "Man Indicted in Rape of Ohio Girl, 10, Who Traveled to Indiana for Abortion." *NBC News*, July 22, 2022. https://www.nbcnews.com/news/us-news/man-indicted-rape-ohio-girl-10-traveled-indiana-abortion-rcna39502.

de Beauvoir, Simone. *The Second Sex*. Translated by Constance Borde and Sheila Malovany-Chevallier. New York: Vintage, 2011.

Dickie, Jane R., et al. "Parent-Child Relationships and Children's Images of God." *Journal for the Scientific Study of Religion* 36 (1997) 25–43. https://doi.org/10.2307/1387880.

Dictionary.com. "Rape Culture." Accessed September 4, 2022. https://www.dictionary.com/browse/rape-culture.

Didion, Joan. *The White Album*. New York: Simon & Schuster, 1979.

Dillmann, A. *Genesis: Critically and Exegetically Expounded*. Translated by Wm. B. Stevenson. Edinburgh: T & T Clark, 1897.

Douglas, Mary. *Natural Symbols: Explorations in Cosmology*. New York: Random House, 1970.

———. *Purity and Danger: An Analysis of Concepts of Pollution and Taboo*. London: Routledge & Kegan Paul, 1966.

Dunn, James D. G. *The Epistles to the Colossians and to Philemon*. Grand Rapids: Eerdmans, 1996.

Eberl, Jason T. "Aquinas on the Nature of Human Beings." *The Review of Metaphysics* 28 (2004) 333–65.

Eden, Dawn. *My Peace I Give You: Healing Sexual Wounds with the Help of the Saints*. Notre Dame, IN: Ave Maria, 2012.

Eliade, Mercia. *Shamanism: Archaic Techniques of Ecstasy.* Princeton, NJ: Princeton University Press, 1964.

Elliott, Dylan. "Flesh and Spirit: The Female Body." In *Medieval Holy Women in the Christian Tradition c. 1100–c. 1500*, edited by A. J. Minnis and Rosalynn Voaden, 13–46. Belgium: Brepols, 2010.

Engberg-Pedersen, Troels. "Stoicism, Platonism, and the Jewishness of Early Christianity." *Oxford University Press* (blog), Sept. 27, 2017. https://blog.oup.com/2017/09/stoicism-platonism-judaism-early-christianity/.

Eriugena, John Scotus. *De Divisione Naturae.* Translated and edited by I. P. Sheldon-Williams and Ludwig Bieler. Dublin: Dublin Institute for Advanced Studies, 1981.

Esposito, Elizabeth. "Embodying Mysticism: The Utilization of Embodied Experience in the Mysticism of Italian Women, Circa 1200–1400 CE." Master's thesis, University of Florida, 2004.

Felitti, Vincent. "The Relation Between Adverse Childhood Experiences and Adult Health: Turning Gold into Lead." *Permanente Journal* 6 (2002) 44–47.

Finkelhor, David, et al. *Sexually Assaulted Children: National Estimates and Characteristics.* Washington, DC: U.S. Department of Justice, 2008. https://www.ojp.gov/pdffiles1/ojjdp/214383.pdf.

Fowler, James. *Faith Development and Pastoral Care.* Philadelphia: Fortress, 1987. Kindle.

Francisco, Clyde. "Genesis: Commentary." In *General Articles: Genesis–Exodus*, 101–288. The Broadman Bible Commentary 1. Rev. ed. Nashville: Broadman, 1969.

Franks, Anne, and John Meteyard. "Liminality: The Transforming Grace of In-Between Places." *Journal of Pastoral Care and Counseling* 61 (2007) 215–22.

Fraser, S. *My Father's House: A Memoir of Incest and Healing.* New York: Harper & Row, 1987.

Fretheim, Terence. "The Book of Genesis: Introduction, Commentary, and Reflections." In *General Articles and Introduction, Commentary, and Reflections for Each Book of the Bible, including the Apocryphal/Deuterocanonical Books: Genesis, Exodus, Leviticus*, 319–674. The New Interpreter's Bible 1. Nashville: Abingdon, 1994.

Gallagher, Shaun. *How the Body Shapes the Mind.* New York: Oxford University Press, 2005.

German School. *The Resurrection of Jesus Christ.* 1750. Oil on canvas, 21½" x 28½." Private collection (formerly Germany).

Getty-Sullivan, Mary Ann. *Women in the New Testament.* Minnesota: Liturgical, 2001.

Gibbs, Raymond W., Jr. *Embodiment and Cognitive Science.* Cambridge: Cambridge University Press, 2005.

Gilfus, Mary. "Women's Experiences of Abuse as Risk Factors for Incarceration." National Electronic Network on Violence Against Women, Dec. 2002. https://vawnet.org/sites/default/files/assets/files/2017-08/AR_Incarceration.pdf.

Gleason, J. J. *Growing Up to God.* New York: Abingdon, 1975.

Gordon, Linda. *Heroes of Their Own Lives: The Politics and History of Family Violence.* Champaign: University of Illinois Press, 2002.

Greenfield, Craig. *Subversive Jesus: An Adventure in Justice, Mercy, and Faithfulness in a Broken World.* Grand Rapids: Zondervan, 2016.

Grenz, Stanley. "Jesus as the Imago Dei: Image of God Christology and Non-Linear Linearity of Theology." *Journal of the Evangelical Theological Society* 47 (2004) 617–28.

Griffiths, Paul J. "Is There a Doctrine of the Descent into Hell?" *Pro-Ecclesia* 17 (2008) 257–68.

Grimm, H. "Luther's Inner Conflict: A Psychological Interpretation." *Cambridge University Press* 4 (1935) 173–86.

Grovijahn, Jane. "A Feminist Theology of Survival: Sexually Abused Women Reclaim Their Broken Bodies as Imago Dei." PhD diss., Graduate Theological Union, 1998.

———. "Theology as an Irruption into Embodiment: Our Need for God." *Theology and Sexuality* 9 (1998) 29–35.

Haberman, Lisa. "The Seduction of Power: An Analogy of Incest and Antebellum Slavery." *Hastings Women's Law Journal* 13 (2002) 307–24.

Heath, Elaine. *We Were the Least of These: Reading the Bible with Survivors of Sexual Abuse*. Grand Rapids: Brazos, 2011.

Hendrix, S. "Luther." In *The Cambridge Companion to Reformation Theology*, edited by D. Bagchi and D. Steinmetz, 39–56. Cambridge: Cambridge University Press, 2004.

Heo, Hye Kyung. *The Liberative Cross: Korean North American Women and the Self-Giving God*. Eugene, OR: Pickwick, 2015.

Herman, Judith. *Trauma and Recovery: The Aftermath of Violence—From Domestic Violence to Political Terror*. New York: Basic, 1997.

Heyward, Carter. *Touching Our Strength: The Erotic as Power and the Love of God*. New York: HarperCollins, 1989.

Hikota, Riyako Cecilia. *And Still We Wait: Hans Urs von Balthasar's Theology of Holy Saturday and Christian Discipleship*. Eugene, OR: Pickwick, 2018.

Hoekema, Anthony A. *Created in God's Image*. Grand Rapids: Eerdmans, 1986.

Hull, William. "John." In *Luke and John*, edited by Clifton J. Allen, 189–376. The Broadman Bible Commentary 9. Nashville: Broadman, 1970.

Hurtig Casbon, Caryl, and Sally Z. Hare. "Bringing the Book to Life: A Reader's and Group Leader's Guide to Exploring Themes in *A Hidden Wholeness*." In *A Hidden Wholeness: The Journey Toward an Undivided Life* by Parker Palmer, 207–58. San Francisco: Jossey-Bass, 2004.

Irenaeus. *Against Heresies*. Translated by Alexander Roberts and William Rambaut. Ante-Nicene Fathers 1. Edited by Alexander Roberts et al. Buffalo, NY: Christian Literature, 1885. Revised and edited by Kevin Knight. http://www.newadvent.org/fathers/0103.htm.

Isherwood, Lisa, and Elizabeth Stuart. *Introducing Body Theology*. Cleveland: Pilgrim, 1998.

James, Frank A. "Thomas Aquinas on Women." *Carolyn Custis James* (blog), Aug. 6, 2013. https://carolyncustisjames.com/2013/08/06/thomas-aquinas-on-women/.

Jechura, Chet Mitchell. "Enfleshing the Erotic: Toward an Embodied Theological Ethic of Human Sexuality." *Theology and Sexuality* 18 (2012) 234–52.

Jerome. *Commentariorum in Epistolam and Ephesios*. Patrologia Latina 26. Edited by J. P. Migne. https://patristica.net/latina/#t026.

———. *Select Letters of St. Jerome*. Translated by E. A. Wright. Cambridge, MA: Harvard University Press, 1963.

John Paul II. *Man and Woman He Created Them: A Theology of the* Body. Translated by Michael Wildstein. Boston: Pauline Books and Media, 2006.

Johnson, Elizabeth. "Naming God She: The Theological Implications." *Boardman Lectureship in Christian Ethics* 5 (2000). https://repository.upenn.edu/boardman/5.

Johnson, Luke Timothy. *The Revelatory Body: Theology as Inductive Art*. Grand Rapids: Eerdmans, 2015.

Jones, Jeannette D. "A Theological Interpretation of 'Viriditas' in Hildegard of Bingen and Gregory the Great." Boston University Department of Musicology and Ethnomusicology, n.d. https://www.bu.edu/pdme/jeannette-jones/.

Jones, Serene. *Trauma and Grace: Theology in a Ruptured World*. Louisville: Westminster John Knox, 2019.

Jonsson, Gunnlaugur. *The Image of God: Genesis 1:26–28 in a Century of Old Testament Research*. Lund: Almqvist and Wiksell, 1988.

Josephus, Flavius. *The Jewish War*. Translated by G. A. Williamson. https://penelope.uchicago.edu/josephus/war-pref.html.

Kaiser, Walter C. "The Book of Leviticus: Introduction, Commentary, and Reflections." In *General and Old Testament Articles; Genesis; Exodus; Leviticus*, edited by Leander E. Keck, 983–1191. The New Interpreter's Bible 1. Nashville: Abingdon, 1994.

Kapic, Kelly. *Embodied Hope: A Theological Meditation on Pain and Suffering*. Downers Grove, IL: InterVarsity, 2017.

Kastner, Josef. *Resurrected Christ*. 20th century, fresco. Döbling Carmelites church, Vienna, Austria.

Keil, C. F., and F. Delitzsch. *Commentary on the Old Testament*. Vol. 1, *The Pentateuch*. Grand Rapids: Eerdmans, 1978.

Kelly, Geffrey B. *Karl Rahner: Theologian of the Graced Search for Meaning*. Edinburgh: T&T Clark, 1993.

Klassen, Chris. *Religion and Popular Culture: A Cultural Studies Approach*. Oxford: Oxford University Press, 2014.

Knight, Jennie S. *Feminist Mysticism and Images of God*. St. Louis: Chalice, 2011.

Kohut, Heinz. *The Analysis of the Self: A Systematic Approach to the Psychoanalytic Treatment of Narcissistic Personality Disorders*. New York: International Universities Press, 1971.

Kovacs, Judith L. *1 Corinthians Interpreted by Early Christian Commentators*. Grand Rapids: Eerdmans, 2005.

Kung, Hans. *Great Christian Thinkers: Paul, Origen, Augustine, Aquinas, Luther, Schleiermacher, Barth*. New York: Continuum, 1994.

Lalumiere, Martin L., et al. *The Causes of Rape: Understanding Individual Differences in Male Propensity for Sexual Aggression*. Washington, DC: American Psychological Association, 2005. Kindle.

Lawrence, Richard T. "Measure the Image of God: The God Image Inventory and the God Image Scales." *Journal of Psychology and Theology* 25 (1997) 214–26.

Levine, Peter. *Waking the Tiger: Healing Trauma*. Berkeley: North Atlantic, 1997.

Lightfoot, J. B. *Saint Paul's Epistles to the Colossians and to Philemon*. Grand Rapids: Zondervan, 1879.

Loftus, E. F. "Planting Misinformation in the Human Mind: A 30 Year Investigation of the Malleability of Memory." *Learning and Memory* 12 (2005) 361–66.

Lorenz, Hendrik. "Ancient Theories of Soul." *The Stanford Encyclopedia of Philosophy*, summer 2009. Edited by Edward Zalta. https://plato.stanford.edu/archives/sum2009/entries/ancient-soul/.

Luther, Martin. *Luther on Creation: A Critical and Devotional Commentary on Genesis*. Edited by John Nicholas Lenker. Minneapolis: Lutherans in All Lands, 1904.

———. *Luther's Works*. Vol. 1, *Lectures on Genesis Chapters*. Edited by Jaroslav Pelikan. St. Louis: Concordia, 1958.

MacQuarrie, John. "Celtic Spirituality." In *Dictionary of Christian Spirituality*, edited by Gordon S. Wakefield, 83–84. Philadelphia: Westminster, 1983.

Martini, Carlo Maria. *On the Body: A Contemporary Theology of the Human Person*. New York: Crossroad, 2001.

Mattox, John Mark. "Augustine: 354–430 CE." *Internet Encyclopedia of Philosophy*. Accessed September 5, 2022. https://iep.utm.edu/augustin/.

McCammon, Sarah, and Becky Sullivan. "Indiana Doctor Says She Has Been Harassed for Giving an Abortion to a 10-Year-Old." NPR, July 26, 2022. https://www.npr.org/2022/07/26/1113577718/indiana-doctor-abortion-ohio-10-year-old.

McCue, J. "'Simul iustus et peccator' in Augustine, Aquinas, and Luther: Toward Putting the Debate in Context." *Oxford Journals* 48 (1980) 81–96.

McDonnell, E. *The Beguines and Beghards in Medieval Culture*. New York: Octagon, 1969.

McFague, Sally. *The Body of God: An Ecological Theology*. Minneapolis: Fortress, 1993.

McKinney Fox, Bethany. *Disability and the Way of Jesus: Holistic Healing in the Gospels and Church*. Downers Grove, IL: IVP Academic, 2019.

Meiring, Jacob. "Theology in the Flesh—Embodied Sensing, Consciousness, and the Mapping of the Body." *Theological Studies* 72 (2016) 1–11.

Messina-Dysert, Gina. *Rape Culture and Spiritual Violence: Religion, Testimony, and Visions of Healing*. London: Routledge, 2015.

Miller, J. Maxwell. "In the Image and Likeness of God." *Journal of Biblical Literature* 91 (1972) 289–304.

Miller-McLemore, Bonnie. "Embodied Knowing, Embodied Theology: What Happened to the Body?" *Pastoral Psychology* 62 (2013) 743–58.

Mintz, Steven. "Placing Childhood Sexual Abuse in Historical Perspective." The Immanent Frame: Secularism, Religion, and the Public Sphere, July 13, 2012. https://tif.ssrc.org/2012/07/13/placing-childhood-sexual-abuse-in-historical-perspective/.

Moder, Ally. "Women, Personhood, and the Male God: A Feminist Critique of Patriarchal Concepts of God in View of Domestic Abuse." *Feminist Theology* 28 (2019) 85–103.

Moltmann-Wendel, Elisabeth. *I Am My Body: A Theology of Embodiment*. New York: Continuum, 1995.

Moore, Gareth. Review of *Sex, Gender and Christian Ethics* by Lisa Sowle Cahil. *Theology and Sexuality* 6 (1999) 115–16.

Moore, Stephen D. *God's Gym: Divine Male Bodies of the Bible*. New York: Routledge, 1996.

Morris, J. E. *Revival of the Gnostic Heresy*. New York: Palgrave Macmillan, 2008.

Mount Shoop, Marcia. "Body-Wise: Refleshing Christian Spiritual Practice in Trauma's Wake." In *Trauma and Transcendence: Suffering and the Limits of Theory*, 240–54. New York: Fordham University Press, 2018.

———. *Let the Bones Dance: Embodiment and the Body of Christ*. Louisville: Westminster John Knox, 2010.

Muessig, Carolyn. "Communities of Discourse: Religious Authority and the Role of Holy Women in the Later Middle Ages." In *Women and Experience in Later Medieval Writing: Reading the Book of Life*, edited by A. Mulder-Bakker and L. McAvoy, 65–82. New York: Palgrave Macmillan, 2009.

National Center for Victims of Crime. "Child Sexual Abuse Statistics." Accessed April 20, 2021. https://victimsofcrime.org/child-sexual-abuse-statistics/.

Nelson, James. *Body Theology.* Louisville: John Knox, 1992.

Northrup, Christiane. *Women's Bodies, Women's Wisdom: Creating Physical and Emotional Health and Healing.* New York: Bantam, 1998.

Pai, A., et al. "Posttraumatic Stress Disorder in the DSM-5: Controversy, Change, and Conceptual Considerations." *Behavioral Sciences* 7 (2017) 7. https://doi.org/10.3390/bs7010007.

Palmer, Parker. *A Hidden Wholeness: The Journey Toward an Undivided Life.* San Francisco: Jossey-Bass, 2004.

Papalia, Nina, et al. "Child Sexual Abuse and Risk of Revictimization: Impact of Child Demographics, Sexual Abuse Characteristics, and Psychiatric Disorders." *Child Maltreatment* 26 (Feb. 2021) 74–86.

Park, Andrew S. *The Wounded Heart of God: The Asian Concept of Han and the Christian Doctrine of Sin.* Nashville: Abingdon, 1993.

Pasnau, Robert. "Saint Thomas Aquinas." *Stanford Encyclopedia of Philosophy*, Summer 2014 edition. Edited by Edward N. Zalta and Uri Nodelman. https://plato.stanford.edu/entries/aquinas/.

Paul, Marla. "How Traumatic Memories Hide in the Brain and How to Retrieve Them." *Northwestern Now*, Aug. 18, 2015. https://news.northwestern.edu/stories/2015/08/traumatic-memories-hide-retrieve-them.

Pearson, Birger A. "Early Christianity and Gnosticism in the History of Religions." *Studia Theologica—Nordic Journal of Theology* 55 (2001) 81–106.

Pelletier Guy, and Lee. C. Handy. "Is Family Dysfunction More Harmful Than Child Sexual Abuse? A Controlled Study." In *Child Sexual Abuse and Adult Offenders: New Theory and Research*, edited by Christopher Bagley and Kanka Mallick, 43–57. London: Routledge, 2018.

Peterson, Eugene. *First and Second Samuel.* Westminster Bible Companion. Louisville: Westminster John Knox, 1999.

Pitstick, Alyssa Lyra. *Light in Darkness: Hans Urs von Balthasar and the Catholic Doctrine of Christ's Descent into Hell.* Grand Rapids: Eerdmans, 2007. Kindle.

Pitstick, Alyssa Lyra, and Edward T. Oakes. "Balthasar, Hell, and Heresy: An Exchange." *First Things*, Dec. 1, 2006. https://www.firstthings.com/article/2006/12/balthasar-hell-and-heresy-an-exchange.

Pleck, Elizabeth. *Domestic Tyranny: The Making of American Social Policy Against Family Violence from Colonial Times to the Present.* Champaign: University of Illinois Press, 2004.

Power, Kim. *Veiled Desire: Augustine on Women.* New York: Continuum, 1996.

Propp, W. H. "Kinship in 2 Samuel 13." *Catholic Biblical Quarterly* 55 (1993) 39–53.

Queensland Brain Institute. "How Are Memories Formed?" Accessed April 20, 2021. https://qbi.uq.edu.au/brain-basics/memory/how-are-memories-formed.

Radford Ruether, Rosemary. "Augustine: Sexuality, Gender, and Women." In *Feminist Interpretations of Augustine*, edited by Judith Chelius Stark, 47–68. Pennsylvania University Press, 2007.

———. *Sexism and God Talk: Toward a Feminist Theology.* Boston: Beacon, 1983.

RAINN. "Children and Teens: Statistics." Accessed April 20, 2021. https://www.rainn.org/statistics/children-and-teens.

Rambo, Shelly. *Spirit and Trauma: A Theology of Remaining.* Louisville: Westminster John Knox, 2010.

Randall, Robert L. "The Legacy of Kohut for Religion and Psychology." *Journal of Religion and Health* 23 (1984) 106–14.

Rasimus, Tuomas, et al. *Stoicism in Early Christianity*. Peabody, MA: Hendrickson, 2010.

Ratzinger, Joseph. *Seek That Which Is Above*. San Francisco: Ignatius, 2007.

Ricci, Carla. *Mary Magdalene and Many Others: Women Who Followed Jesus*. Minneapolis: Fortress, 1994.

Ridderbos, Herman. *Paul: An Outline of His Theology*. Translated by John Richard de Witt. Grand Rapids: Eerdmans, 1975.

Rizzuto, Ana-Maria. *Birth of the Living God: A Psychoanalytic Study*. Chicago: University of Chicago Press, 1979.

Robertson, Stephen. "Age of Consent Laws." Children and Youth in History. Accessed November 3, 2021. https://chnm.gmu.edu/cyh/teaching-modules/230.html.

———. *Crimes Against Children: Sexual Violence and Legal Culture in New York City, 1880–1960*. Chapel Hill: University of North Carolina Press, 2005.

Robinson, Gnana. *1 and 2 Samuel: Let Us Be Like the Nations*. Grand Rapids: Eerdmans, 1993.

Rohr, Richard. *Everything Belongs: The Gift of Contemplative Prayer*. New York: Crossroad, 2003.

Rosen, Andrew. "What Is Trauma." The Center for Treatment of Anxiety and Mood Disorders. Last modified September 25, 2018. https://centerforanxietydisorders.com/what-is-trauma/.

Ruffing, Janet K. *Spiritual Direction: Beyond the Beginnings*. New York: Paulist, 2000.

Sadler, Raleigh. *Vulnerability: Rethinking Human Trafficking*. Nashville: B&H, 2019.

Saha, Formila, et al. "A Narrative Exploration of the Sense of Self of Women Recovering from Childhood Sexual Abuse." *Counselling Psychology Quarterly* 24 (2011) 101–13.

Saward, John. *The Mysteries of March: Hans Urs von Balthasar on the Incarnation and Easter*. New York: HarperCollins, 1990.

Scarry, Elaine. *The Body in Pain: Making and Unmaking of the World*. Oxford: Oxford University Press, 1985.

Schüssler Fiorenza, Elisabeth. *But She Said: Feminist Practices of Biblical Interpretation*. Boston: Beacon, 1992.

———. *In Memory of Her: A Feminist Theological Reconstruction of Christian Origins*. New York: Herder & Herder, 1994.

———. *Wisdom Ways: Introduction Feminist Biblical Interpretation*. Maryknoll, NY: Orbis, 1970.

Shapiro, Fred R., ed. *The New Yale Book of Quotations*. New Haven: Yale University Press, 2021.

Shooter, Susan. *How Survivors of Abuse Relate to God: The Authentic Spirituality of the Annihilated Soul*. London: Routledge, 2012.

Simango, Daniel. "The Imago Dei (Gen 1:26–27): A History of Interpretation from Philo to the Present." *Studie Historiae Ecclesiasticae* 42 (2016) 172–90.

Sloyan, Gerard S. *The Crucifixion of Jesus: History, Myth, Faith*. Minneapolis: Fortress, 1995.

Smith, Shanell T. "'This Is My Body': A Womanist Reflection on Jesus' Sexualized Trauma During His Crucifixion from a Survivor of Sexual Assault." In *When Did We See You Naked: Jesus as a Victim of Sexual Abuse*, edited by Jayme R. Reaves et al., 278–86 London: SCM, 2021.

Snyder, Howard N. *Sexual Assault of Young Children as Reported to Law Enforcement: Victim, Incident, and Offender Characteristics*. Washington, DC: U.S. Department of Justice, 2000. https://www.bjs.gov/content/pub/pdf/saycrle.pdf.

Soliman, Tamer M., et al. "It's Not 'All in Your Head': Understanding Religion from an Embodied Cognition Perspective." *Perspectives on Psychological Science* 10 (2015) 852–64.

Sölle, Dorothee. "Fatherhood, Power, and Barbarism: Feminist Challenges to Authoritarian Religion." In *Eerdmans Reader to Contemporary Political Theology*, edited by William Cavanaugh et al., 327–36. Grand Rapids: Eerdmans, 2012.

Stagg, Frank. "Matthew." In *General Articles: Matthew–Mark*, edited by Clifton J. Allen, 61–253. The Broadman Bible Commentary 8. Nashville: Broadman, 1969.

Strauss, Mark. *Four Portraits, One Jesus: A Survey of Jesus and the Gospels*. Grand Rapids: Zondervan, 2007.

Strozier, Charles. *Heinz Kohut: The Making of a Psychoanalyst*. New York: Farrar, Straus and Giroux, 2001.

Tamayo, A., and L. Desjardins. "Belief Systems and Conceptual Images of Parents and God." *Journal of Psychology* 92 (1976) 131–40.

Tertullian. "On the Apparel of Women." Book 1. Translated by S. Thelwall. Ante-Nicene Fathers 4. Edited by Alexander Roberts et al. Buffalo, NY: Christian Literature, 1885. Revised and edited by Kevin Knight. https://www.newadvent.org/fathers/0402.htm.

Thomas Aquinas. *The Summa Theologica*. Great Books of the Western World 19 and 20. Edited by Robert Maynard Hutchins. London: William Benton, 1952.

———. *Summa Theologica*. Translated by Fathers of the English Dominican Province. Edited by Kevin Knight. 2017. https://www.newadvent.org/summa/.

Tombs, David. "Crucifixion and Sexual Abuse." In *When Did We See You Naked? Jesus as a Victim of Sexual Abuse*, edited by Jayme Reaves et al., 15–27 London: SCM, 2021.

Torjesen, Karen Jo. *When Women Were Priests: Women's Leadership in the Early Church and the Scandal of Their Subordination in the Rise of Christianity*. New York: Harper San Francisco, 1993.

Tracy, David. *Analogical Imagination: Christian Theology and the Culture of Pluralism*. New York: Crossroad, 1989.

Trexler, Richard. *Sex and Conquest: Gendered Violence, Political Order, and the European Conquest of the Americas*. Cambridge: Polity, 1995.

van der Kolk, Bessel. "The Body Keeps the Score: Integration of Body and Mind in the Treatment of Traumatized People." Lecture at The Trauma Center, Brookline, MA, January 24, 2007.

———. *The Body Keeps the Score: Brain, Mind, and Body in the Healing of Trauma*. New York: Penguin, 2014.

Vergote, A. "Concept of God and Parental Images." *Journal for the Scientific Study of Religions* 8 (1969) 79–87.

Voelkel, Rebecca. *Carnal Knowledge of God: Embodied Love and the Movement for Justice*. Minneapolis: Fortress, 2017.

Vorster, N. "Calvin's Modification of Augustine's Doctrine of Original Sin." *In die Skriflig/In Luce Verbi* 44 (2010) 71–89.

Weems, Renita. *Battered Love: Marriage, Sex, and Violence in the Hebrew Prophets*. Minneapolis: Fortress, 1995.

Wei, Ian. *Intellectual Culture in Medieval Paris: Theologians and the University*. Cambridge: Cambridge University Press, 2012.

Weinandy, Thomas. "St. Irenaeus and the *Imago Dei:* The Importance of Being Human." *Logos* 6 (2003) 15–34.

Weiss, J., et al. "A Study of Girl Sex Victims." *Psychiatric Quarterly* 29 (1955) 1–27.

West, Stuart. "The Rape of Dinah and the Conquest of Shechem." *Dor le Dor* 8 (1980) 144–56.

Westermann, C. *Genesis 1–11: A Commentary.* Minneapolis: Augsburg, 1987.

White, W. A. *The Mental Hygiene of Childhood.* Boston: Little, Brown, 1919.

Winnicott, D. W. "Transitional Objects and Transitional Phenomena." *International Journal of Psychoanalysis* 34 (1953) 89–97.

Winston, Robert, and Rebecca Chicot. "The Importance of Early-Bonding on the Long Term Mental Health and Resilience of Children." *London Journal of Primary Care* 8 (2016) 12–14.

The Women of Magdalene, and Becca Stevens. *Find Your Way Home: Words from the Street, Wisdom from the Heart.* Nashville: Abingdon, 2008.

Woodruff, Alan. "What Is a Neuron?" Queensland Brain Institute. Accessed April 20, 2021. https://qbi.uq.edu.au/brain/brain-anatomy/what-neuron.

Wright, N. T. "Did Jesus Really Rise from the Dead?" Lecture at the Bast Center, Roanoke College, Salem, VA, March 16, 2007. https://youtu.be/KnkNKIJ_dnw.

———. *Resurrection of the Son of God.* Vol. 3 of *Christian Origins and the Son of God.* Minneapolis: Fortress, 2003.

———. *Surprised by Hope: Rethinking Heaven, the Resurrection, and the Mission of the Church.* New York: HarperCollins, 2009.

Wurthwein, Ernst. *The Text of the Old Testament.* London: SCM, 1989.

Youssef. "Sour Wine and Gall: Was It a Merciful Gesture or Mockery?" Coptic Orthodox Diocese of the Southern United States, Apr. 19, 2008. https://suscopts.org/resources/literature/542/sour-wine-and-gall-was-it-a-merciful-gesture-or-mo/.

# Index

www.ingramcontent.com/pod-product-compliance
Lightning Source LLC
LaVergne TN
LVHW050646100826
845148LV00011B/1997

* 9 7 9 8 3 8 5 2 1 0 1 3 8 *